MANAGEMENT
WITHOUT TEARS

James O. McDonald

MANAGEMENT WITHOUT TEARS:

A Guide to Coping with Everyday Organizational Problems

SPHERE REFERENCE

Sphere Reference
27 Wrights Lane
London
W8 5TZ

First published by Crain Books
A Division of Crain Communications, Inc.
740 Rush Street, Chicago, IL 60611
Copyright © 1981 by James O. McDonald
Published by Sphere Books Ltd 1987

Photoset by Rowland Phototypesetting Ltd,
Bury St Edmunds, Suffolk
Printed by William Collins Sons & Co. Ltd., Glasgow

To Dale Bryson for the idea

To Mary, my wife, for her help and encouragement

Contents

Acknowledgments

The raw material for this book was provided in generous portions by those persons I have known and worked with most closely. Intentionally or not, they taught me how to manage. To them, I owe everlasting thanks.

Some persons taught me more than others, but each taught me something. To single out but a few of my leading teachers, I would surely have to name Lida Usilton, Kenny Revelle, Wally Poston, Frank Corrado, Larry Smith, John Quarles, Joel Mintz, Andy Damen, Alan Kirk, and Olive Weeks. And then there are Tom Yeates, Murray Stein, Dave Ullrich, George Alexander, Lance Vinson, David Comey, Dale Bryson, Carol Foglesong, and Tom Sullivan. Some were my bosses, others worked for me, and still others were colleagues or critics. First and foremost, though, in the give and take that comprises the fascinating world of management, I learned from them.

Through it all, my wife Mary, a great teacher, has always been there to keep me on course when the sailing got rough. Her support has been boundless.

In their own ways, they all made this book possible.

Introduction

When I became a manager for the first time, I was struck by how little I knew about effectively handling people and things. I quickly learned that being a manager was entirely different from being a nonmanagerial employee in the same organization. As I floundered through that early experience, I was surprised at the paucity of practical 'how-to' books and training courses for managers. Nowhere did I find that special book of suggestions written by an experienced manager, although I did find many treatises and books written by academics and management consultants. What I needed at the time, however, was a practical step-by-step guide on how to manage specific situations, written by someone who had struggled through the management hierarchy. I wanted something compact I could refer to when I faced a new problem. Now after years of managerial experience, I decided to write this book to provide the information I sought long ago but couldn't find.

The secret of being a successful manager is having the ability to get things done. Since managers get things done almost entirely through others, they must develop techniques to make sure that others do, indeed, get things done. A manager must harness the use of his time, so that he can spend most of that time managing, which means planning what needs to be done and implementing his plans through those he manages. This book discloses the managerial methods I used. I refined these methods over the years in actual on-the-job managerial settings, and because the methods worked well for me, I want to share them with you to help make your managerial life more productive and rewarding, wherever you may be on the managerial ladder.

The book sets forth some managerial problems likely to be encountered during the career of a manager. Each problem is followed by at least one suggested solution. Being able to pick the best solution more often than not is what separates a good manager from a so-so one, and, as any seasoned manager knows, there is more than one solution for any problem. The solutions presented in this book worked best for me and for those who trained under me. If they are properly understood and applied, I believe they can work as well for you.

A Good Word for Good Work

'There is something that is much more scarce, something rarer than ability. It is the ability to recognize ability.'

Robert Half

Problem: The only time Susan got any word back from the boss on the quality of her work was when she did something that wasn't up to par. Then he was quick to let her know about her shortcomings. Although she knew that her work was generally above average and sometimes even superlative, the boss never once praised her performance. She didn't expect a continuing stream of praise, but she did think that occasional recognition for an outstanding job was warranted. After all, she thought, what does it take to get some praise around here?

Approach: Susan's boss has forgotten that each of us, including him, likes a reward for a job well done. From a dollars and cents standpoint, the best reward is a promotion with a rise in salary, responsibility, and prestige. But no matter how outstanding we may be as employees, promotions come along relatively seldom. Still, a boss can reward an employee with meaningful recognition by simply voicing a compliment when it is merited.

For example, if an employee submits an exceptionally good piece of work, take time out to express your satisfaction. A hand-written note on the file copy or on a memo, such as, 'Excellent job, Susan – clear, concise, and responsive. *Keep it up!*' is a real morale builder. So that others understand what you consider an exceptional job, route the note back to the employee through the supervisory chain. That way, you'll give a message to a number of people. You'll demonstrate the type of work standards that you seek. Mostly, though, a personal pat on the back from the boss serves as motivation for future good work.

The value that one former employee of mine attached to such notes was impressed upon me when I met him several years after I changed jobs. He told me that because his present boss never praised him, he would periodically pull out my old notes of encouragement and read them when he needed to boost his sagging spirits.

This pat-on-the-back type of note need not be restricted only to those employees who turn in outstanding performances. The same technique ('Tom, this is a *great* improvement over your last effort – fewer words, more substance, and on time') can be used to encourage an employee who shows improvement over his usual 'average' performance.

About the Office Machine Game

'Those who speak most of progress measure it by quantity and not quality.' ·

George Santayana

Problem: On Mac's first inspection tour of the office after he became director, he noticed that the office was crowded with latest-model office machines. He noticed, also, that few of the machines were actually in operation. The staff was busy, but the machines were not. Within a week his secretary presented him with a request to purchase several costly office machines. No justification was attached to the purchase request.

Approach: Lesson number one for Mac: Office machines are outdated the day they are purchased. Sales techniques for office machines are analogous to those of cars. This results in constant pressure on the manager to buy the new improved models.

The pressure to buy comes from the salespeople who visit your organization regularly, from the purchasing department personnel who develop congenial relationships with the salespeople, and from employees who have learned about the wonderful new machines not yet possessed by your office. Pressures also develop within your own staff to acquire additional models of machines you already possess so that more of the staff will have access to them. Decisions on machine purchases can rank among the most expensive budget decisions that a manager encounters.

If the decision to acquire or not to acquire an office machine is not under your direct control, take steps to get it there. Failing that, involve yourself to the extent that you can. There are numerous questions to be answered before you can make an intelligent decision about the purchase of a machine. Some of these are:

1. What benefits will result from the purchase of the machine?
2. Are these benefits needed in your office?
3. Will your goals be met more readily if the machine is available?
4. Can your budget afford it?
5. What are the maintenance costs?
6. If you acquire this machine, are you setting the stage to acquire others?
7. What experiences have other offices had with the machine?

(Disregard the salesperson's pitch and contact the supervisors in those other offices.)

8. How much staff training is required to operate the machine?
9. Is your office space conducive to housing this machine? (Some machines require climate control and special lighting and electrical connections.)
10. Is the machine already obsolete? If not, when will it be? What's on the drawing board to replace it?
11. Is there enough work to fully use the machine?
12. Are similar machines in your office now being fully used?

If you require not only completion of such a checklist, but also verification of the information before you consider purchase of an office machine, you insert a degree of integrity into the purchasing process. If you let the salespeople, the purchasing agents, and the staff know that you are personally interested in this machine acquisition, you influence the quality of information fed to you for making the decision. The influence becomes even greater if you also establish procedures for periodic evaluations of the use, maintenance costs, benefits, training, and validation of prepurchase claims for the machines.

The trap to side-step is that of being persuaded to buy a machine just because it's a new product for which the salesperson claims fantastic performance. Even if his claims are true but don't suit your needs, your checklist will give you a logical basis for deciding against the purchase.

Assisting the New Supervisor

'The brighter you are, the more you have to learn.'
Don Herold

Problem: Anita's first week as a supervisor gave her a sinking feeling. She hadn't bargained for the types of problems that arose. She reflected that during the job interview her boss had not clearly outlined the full breadth of her managerial responsibilities. If he had done so, at least she would have known what to expect. One of the things that affected her most was the loneliness of the decision-making process. In making decisions, there seemed to be no one on her staff to whom she could turn for a straight answer. She hesitated to discuss her worries with her boss because she feared he might view them as a sign of weakness.

Approach: Being promoted from a position as staff employee with no supervisory responsibilities to a supervisory position is like going from bachelorhood to marriage. You look the same, but you don't feel the same. Your status has changed. To some, as Anita discovered, instead of being a pleasure, promotion turns out to be an agonizing experience.

Good managers are always on the lookout for other potentially good managers. It's normal to urge an outstanding nonsupervisory employee to fill a vacant managerial spot. However, being an outstanding nonsupervisory employee does not guarantee success as a supervisor. A staff employee is responsible only for her own affairs. She can go as fast as her capabilities, her desires, and, perhaps, her supervisor permit. Administrative worries pertaining to budgets, personnel, data processing, travel, purchasing, and planning are limited or nonexistent for a nonsupervisor.

The supervisor's world is different. The primary mission is to get things done through others. To a new supervisor, the inability to personally see a project through from start to finish becomes dramatically evident from the first day on the job. The new supervisor discovers that being an outstanding engineer or a superb accountant is of little help to handle the problem of a chronically tardy employee, or to insure that next year's budget reflects projected needs, or to justify the purchase of a new copying machine, or to process a customer's complaint with dispatch. The sudden change in responsibilities can readily result in feelings of helplessness and confusion while the new manager adjusts to this new status.

You can soften the impact of the change for an inexperienced supervisor under your jurisdiction if, during the interview and selection process, for example, you candidly discuss the frustrations, as well

5

as the joys, of the supervisory world. Explain the different requirements of supervisory work, compared with those of the present nonsupervisory job. Explore the standards of performance by which she, as a supervisor, will be judged. Tell her of available supervisory training courses. It is most important to assure her that you will provide all possible help, especially during the first days on the new job. Be elemental and tell her that if she feels lost and uncertain at first, she is experiencing a normal reaction. Make it clear that you want the new manager to succeed and will help her if only because your success is closely allied to hers. Explain that not only do you encourage her to come to you to discuss managerial problems, but you will also hold monthly sessions with her in which the two of you will review her progress.

Establishing this kind of working relationship with the new supervisor before her entry on the job will fortify her with support and confidence that might otherwise be lacking. Any dividends she reaps from your help will be reaped by you, also.

Bridging the Gap

'Leadership is action, not position.'
Donald H. McGannon

Problem: Jeff's return to the office from his first long holiday since becoming chief of the division was a revelation. The pile of unsigned letters, the unanswered telephone calls, the unapproved documents all waiting for his action made him wonder if he'd ever catch up. After that, he was reluctant to leave the office, even though his position required extended travel from time to time. Most of the items awaiting action by him appeared to be legitimate enough. A number of the unsigned letters had notes from the originators saying, 'Please hold for Jeff's signature,' and several of the telephone messages said 'Caller wants to speak to Jeff, only.'

Approach: Does taking a two-week holiday from your busy office conjure up such an agonizing picture of the work that will be waiting upon your return that the holiday seems hardly worth taking? Dreading the return to the pile-up in the office can build up to the point that the benefits of a holiday are destroyed. Who said you have to endure this form of torture? You said so – that's who – because you did not install a system to circumvent the problem.

It's your own fault if you return to a work place mired in a backlog. You sow the seeds of the backlog when you fail to develop a system of management continuity in your absence. So, right now, before you face such a backlog again, work out the procedures to control the flow of work in your absence and insist that they be followed whenever you are out of the office, whether for a holiday, business, or illness.

As part of your office continuity procedures, develop a chain of command for someone to act in your *full* stead while you are not in the office. *Full* stead means full stead. That idea has to be accepted completely by everyone, including the person acting in your place. That person works on everything that you would work on if you were there: signing correspondence, delegating work, answering calls, making decisions, the whole bit. He holds nothing for your return unless you so instruct. Not only do you feel better when you return to a clean desk, but you also feel virtuous because when you delegate authority this way, you are developing your subordinates, thereby strengthening the operation of your office. It's a vote of confidence to those left behind. And it's a vote of relief for you.

Bon voyage! Have a good trip.

Budget Tracking

'When it is a question of money, everybody is of the same religion.'

Voltaire

Problem: Owen's bookkeeper kept an elaborate set of books on the finances of the organization. As the budget year progressed, some units under Owen's supervision underspent their budgeted funds and others overspent. Because of the detailed nature of the book-keeping system, Owen did not receive timely reports of such under- and overexpenditures in spite of his repeated requests. When the reports finally did reach him, they were so detailed that Owen didn't want to read them. As far as he was concerned, keeping timely track of the budget was strictly a hit-or-miss operation.

Approach: Getting enough money each year to run an organization is a condition necessary to the continuation of the organization. Once the funds are allocated, keeping within the budget can be an exasperating job unless the manager establishes expenditure controls. Not staying within your budget generates disagreeable events, including redundancies, restricting necessary travel, and losing unspent money that could have been used elsewhere. As a result, the budget begins to take you over. Owen may well be heading in such a direction.

When you secure the funds to run an organization, you are at the end of one effort and at the beginning of another. You have to know what you've spent in purchases and in fixed expenses in relation to how much of the year has elapsed so that you can determine whether you're underspending or overspending. Once you have made this determination, you can take action to get back on schedule. Sounds simple enough.

To manage your money properly, you have to track your budget closely. The simpler the system for doing this, the more quickly and easily you'll be able to detect the need for corrective action. If you design a tracking system that is so detailed that it can be understood only by a professional accountant, it will be of little use to you even if you happen to be a trained accountant. Although you may understand the system yourself, others may not be able to. Therefore, keep it simple, and, as you receive reports, you can pass them on to others on your staff.

A good budget-tracking system is a single-page monthly report for each unit listing the following information for at least salary, travel, and all other projected expenses:

1.	the total amount of money available for the year.
2.	the percentage of the annual budget spent during the month just ended.
3.	the cumulative percentage of the available funds spent to date for the entire year.
4.	the cumulative percentages that should have been spent by now if expenditures were right on schedule.

Getting this type of summary tracking report on your desk no later than five days after the close of each month will give you the information you need to track your budget. Within sixty seconds after you receive the report, you can determine where you stand in relation to the budget. Followup action can then be taken to shore up soft spots.

You may have a problem in starting a simple tracking system. Accountants and bookkeepers love to deal in details. Every penny is important to them in balancing the books. They like to present you with detailed reports instead of one in the easy-to-read, one-page format I've outlined. But persist until you finally get what you need. That's the day you'll gain control of the budget. Until you have your budget under control, you aren't truly in a position to run your organization.

Catching Up

'I shall tell you a great secret, my friend. Do not wait for the last judgment. It takes place every day.'
                                                        Albert Camus

Problem: Important events naturally continued to occur in the office when Albert, the section chief, was away on a business trip or on a holiday. After he returned, his staff tried to inform him verbally about what transpired during his absence, but their summaries were not complete. Members of his staff themselves were frequently out of the office on trips when he returned, so they were unable to discuss the events at that time, which was when he needed to know about them. Sometimes the staff forgot important items, and sometimes they didn't recognize which developments were important. The longer the time Albert was absent from the office, the less effective were the attempts to keep him briefed. In his short time as section chief, he had already experienced several setbacks because he had not been informed of crucial events that had happened in his absence.

Approach: Albert faces a problem common to all managers. A manager's absence from the office, whether due to travel, sickness, or holiday, creates a gap in his knowledge of office affairs. Although you may have taken steps to insure that the office functions fully in your absence, the absence itself creates problems for you. These problems can be caused by your lack of knowledge of any of a number of occurrences that can influence future decisions. These could be your lack of knowledge about a policy change, an external development, or a personnel problem. Anything can happen in your absence, and, for one reason or another, you may not learn about it until too late. Fortunately, you can erect safeguards to keep on top of developments that occur while you are away, rather than leave the coverage of such developments to chance.

Keeping track of incoming and outgoing letters, memos, and reports that you would have seen if you were in the office is a relatively easy matter. Instruct your secretary to make an extra copy of each for you. You can thumb through these quickly, pulling those you want to raise questions about or study in more detail. Make this procedure routine to cover any of your absences, even for as short a period as a day, whether your absence is due to travel, illness, or holiday.

For items not covered by the extra copy procedure, instruct the person acting in your stead to furnish you with copies of memoranda of those phone calls you ought to be aware of. In addition, ask him to dictate a brief summary, with topical headings like newspaper headlines, of other information you need to know. This system will help protect you from being taken unawares by subsequent events resulting from those that occurred while you were away.

Be sure that your procedure includes instruction that all of these briefing materials be deposited on your desk in a folder at the end of the last business day before you are scheduled to return to the office. When you return, you can sort through the material before your work day gets underway. If you've been away from the office for an extended period, you may want to drop in the night before, or during the weekend before your return to the office to review events that occurred while you were gone.

When you set up these types of procedures, you'll probably feel overwhelmed by the sheer volume of briefing material that greets you after a long holiday or business trip. The off-hours return on the night before or the weekend before helps to overcome that buried feeling by giving you a headstart, so you can resume your normal working habits immediately.

Changing Directions

'Crank – a man with a new idea until it succeeds.'
Mark Twain

Problem: Mike was dissatisfied with his staff's accomplishments. He knew the staff was capable, busy, and well motivated. Yet they consistently fell short of the types of major accomplishments that make people sit up and take notice. Mike wondered what tack he should take to change course. He had tried the reorganization route, and it did not provide the answer. What he really wanted was to institute changes that would make better use of his staff's capabilities and produce dramatic improvements.

Approach: Mike might eventually learn that the infusion of a major new idea from the top can produce an essentially brand new organization. The beauty of such a move is that the manager can change the organization without prolonged studies, reports, committees, or reorganizations.

How one idea can switch the direction of an organization was demonstrated to me by one of my bosses while I was working for the government some years ago. Government regulations required industries and municipalities to meet certain pollution-control standards. Until the new boss's arrival – from the private sector – our agency representatives would discuss the alleged violation with representatives of the polluter. In many cases, it seemed these negotiations went on endlessly as we tried to get them to agree to install pollution-control devices. Usually, the agency would bring suit against a violator only if he refused to install such devices. The violators knew this was the custom of the agency, and many of the more recalcitrant ones did their utmost to drag out the negotiations, thus saving money because they postponed the time when capital expenditures had to be made to install pollution-control devices.

Enter the new boss. Enter a new idea almost overnight. The new idea? A simple one, understandable by both the agency and the violators. Instead of trying to negotiate a settlement first (and often failing to reach a settlement at all), the new boss reversed the process by filing the lawsuit first and then negotiating.

The effects of this policy switch were enormous. No one likes to be sued. Business, in particular, abhors lawsuits because of adverse publicity, complaints from shareholders, impact on earnings, and the cost of defending the suit, not to mention the possibility that corporate officials might have to testify in court. Being sued is not a pleasant experience. If there is a solid case, the filing of a lawsuit has a tendency to hasten the settlement, rather than string it out in negotiations prior to the filing of a suit. So my new boss maximized his leverage for getting things done by _____ a relatively simple idea. He also swiftly put his personal se_____ _____rk methods of the organization.

My new boss se_____ a basic change in the organization without the change _____ _____ganizational box. Because he forced the filing of large numb_____ _____ he also forced an internal restructuring of the skills needed _____ he trial of those suits; he helped shorten negotiating time, _____ _____ d the design of intensive training programmes to acquire the _____ needed to implement his new idea.

A new idea is not a total so_____ _____roblem. It is one step in the process of solving a problem. P_____ _____ shepherding the new idea through to a conclusion is a mus_____ _____ up the systems to make the idea work is mandatory. Overcon_____ resistance to the new idea requires hard work from the beginning. The idea has to be sufficiently well conceived so that problems as well as benefits are anticipated.

If you spot the problems, while also concluding that the new idea constitutes a valuable contribution towards getting things done better, implementation of your new idea will reconstruct the face of your organization. The gains can be considerable. Put on your thinking cap to come up with that one major new idea that can awaken your organization to exciting possibilities for getting things done. Start by itemizing those things about your work that dissatisfy you the most and come exclusively under your control, so that you can institute a change without the delay involved in getting approval from others. Then think big, really big, in coming up with a realistic solution to your single biggest dissatisfaction among those you've listed. Look for the solution that promises a dramatic, yet relatively simple, turnaround of that prime dissatisfaction, and you are on your way to a change in direction. When you have succeeded with that problem, start to work on the next, and so on down the list. You will be amazed at how easily you can eliminate some of your worst headaches by this method.

Coffee Breaks

'We are confronted by a condition, not a theory.'
Grover Cleveland

Problem: Mayme had been an employee long enough to know that
employees frequently extend their coffee breaks beyond the official
time limit. Other than occasional outbursts to condemn this practice,
management did nothing to stop the abuses. Now that Mayme herself
was a manager, she worried about the time wasted on excessively long
breaks. She was trying hard to increase the productivity of her unit, so
she was determined to remedy coffee break abuse even though other
managers had practically given up trying to do so.

Approach: Mayme must realize that the coffee break is here to stay.
Recognizing that she has to live with it may help her to devise a
practical plan to diminish employee abuse of the break.

Potential solutions to this managerial problem are numerous.
A workable solution to be applied to the problem in any one office
is unique to that office and depends on many factors, such as the
number of employees, the nature of their occupations, the attitude of
management.

If you have Mayme's problem, here are some suggestions to remedy
it. First, consider the number of employees under your jurisdiction. If
there are only a few, do the obvious and give them a personal admoni-
tion, either verbal or written, to limit the break to the allocated time.

Some offices with many employees have tried a system of bells that
toll the start and end of each coffee break as well as signal the times of
the beginning and ending of the lunch period and the work day.
Supervisors are expected to observe whether their employees respond
to the coffee break bells and take appropriate action if too many
employees ignore them. While this bell system may appear somewhat
harsh if you're not familiar with it, it does serve to indicate the
significant times of a work day in an impersonal manner. If the
installation of a bell system does not appeal to you or your staff, borrow
the other part of the remedy and assign to each supervisor the duty of
policing the subordinates' coffee break behaviour.

Another method of control is to adopt a check-out/check-in system
for breaks. If a time clock is not available, this method requires that a
monitor be appointed for the sign-out/sign-in sheet. Here again the
supervisor is accountable if the employees abuse the break privilege.

A system that does not require travel time to and from a restaurant is
to install vending machines that dispense coffee, tea, chocolate, and

soup. Since these machines are maintained by a concessionaire, there is no management responsibility to keep them in working order.

Another system to eliminate travel time is that in which management installs electric coffee makers in the office and provides free or inexpensive coffee to the employees. Whoever happens to be near the machine makes a new pot of coffee when the last one is nearly empty. It takes time and funds to maintain this system satisfactorily: coffee, tea, chocolate, milk and sugar must be purchased and kept available at each machine; machines and glass pots must be replaced fairly regularly, since both are easily damaged; and an occasional thorough clean-up in the areas around the machines is necessary. So if you opt for this solution, make ample provision in advance for these maintenance and supply requirements. You can thus prevent the headaches of KP assignments after the novelty of the office coffee wears off.

No matter what solution you select, expect to remind your employees from time to time to keep their coffee breaks within the prescribed time limits. For some reason, no one retains this rule in memory for very long, no matter how irritated you may get over its infraction. And managers, with so many demands on their own time, develop acute sensitivity to coffee break abuses.

As you mull over these and the other possible solutions to the problem, there is one you really should not even consider. That is the idea of doing away with the coffee break. This 'cure', if you selected it, would tab you as reckless, a manager with no regard for his chin. You would be punchy as the attacks came from all sides, and your employee relations would completely disintegrate. Aside from the employee disgruntlement abolition would cause, common sense should tell you that the break really is generally beneficial to workers. It provides temporary diversion for their minds and mild exercise for their bodies. Both of these benefits can be reflected in their work after break time. It may help soothe your managerial nerves to realize that work is the main topic discussed by employees during their breaks. Solutions to problems are often exchanged, and the result can be smoother operation in your office when these solutions are adopted by your employees.

Committees

*'You'll find in no park or city
A monument to a committee.'*
Victoria Pasternak

Problem: Whenever John needed to consult with either Tab or Lloyd, two of his middle-level employees, he was all too often told that 'He's at a committee meeting'. Since both employees frequently failed to meet deadlines in their work assignments, John finally suggested to them that more time spent on their official work and less on attendance at committee meetings might help improve their deadline situation. But they disagreed and insisted that their work on committees was of significant importance both to their own work and to that of the organization.

Approach: If, like John, you find that members of your staff seem to be heavily burdened with work from committees on which they serve, consider taking inventory of those committees and learning more about them. Start by listing the names of the committees – their types, what purposes they serve, who created them, when they were created, why they were created, their termination dates (if any), who has the authority to dissolve them, how many members serve on each, how many of your employees are on each, how effective your employees are on their committees, how much time each meeting consumes and how often, how much it costs your office to have your employees serve.

To complete your research, you will have to consult managers of other divisions for data on those committees outside your managerial control. They can tell you, for instance, the value of their committees and just how much your employees contribute as members. Get an evaluation of those committees' effectiveness from each employee in your office who serves on them. Incidentally, if you are not already doing so, require each of your employees on these outside committees to submit to you a report of each meeting he attends and continue this practice even after your study is complete. For the committees under your jurisdiction, consult the regular summaries you receive from the committee head after each meeting and analyse the worth of the committees. Get a candid opinion from some of the members of your staff, too.

When you have assembled all the data, you can assess the value of each committee on which you or any of your employees serve. For each committee, decide the following: What benefit does the parent organization derive? What benefit does your own office derive? Is there

16

a better way to secure this benefit? Is the benefit worth the cost of the time expended by your employees? If it is within your power to dissolve this committee, should you do so? If it is not within your power, should you make an effort to have it dissolved? Would the committee be more effective if it were enlarged? diminished? composed of different persons?

To formulate a sensible conclusion, you should decide also on the following points: Do you see a need for any additional committees to be created at this time? Are committee assignments concentrated on only a few of your employees? Should more of them be asked to serve?

From the answers to these questions, you'll be able to draw valuable conclusions about the worth of the committees that involve you and your office staff. Organizations differ so in character and in the number and value of their committees that no one can prognosticate just what your conclusions will be. But your newly acquired knowledge about the committees closest to you should serve you in good stead. You'll be better able to respond when an employee tells you he has to take more time for his committee work. You may even be able to retrieve some of your employees from their current committee assignments and put them to work again on your department's goals.

You can, and probably will, delegate the spade work for committee research to someone on your staff. But, please, try not to appoint a committee to make the study!

Completed Staff Work

*'When you get right down to the root of the meaning
of the word "succeed", you find that it simply means
to follow through.'*

F. W. Nichol

Problem: Sheila had a good education, a varied background, and a
pleasant disposition. She was bright. But she hesitated to finish any
assignment without first trying to find out exactly what the boss
wanted in the completed product. Whenever she couldn't get in to see
him, she wrote a note to ask his views on whether she was progressing
on the right track. All of this quest for direction took a lot of time, but
Sheila felt better to think that she had pleased the boss. The boss didn't
appreciate Sheila's frequent quizzes, but he wasn't sure how to tell her
without hurting her feelings.

Approach: Sheila is not alone in her search for direction. Many an
employee, and not only the inexperienced, feels the need to discuss an
assignment with the boss or to submit a rough draft of a proposed
completion of an assignment. The more difficult the assignment, the
more the employee tends to present the solution piecemeal. The
employee is not only uncertain of himself, he's uncertain about how to
perform his job. He wants to 'please' the boss with the 'right' solution.
Even the most capable employee can fall into such behaviour patterns if
the boss encourages this approach to problem solving.

To overcome this tendency and to promote staff development, let
your staff know that you subscribe to the doctrine of 'completed staff
work'. This means that each staff member studies his assignment and
then presents a solution or a finished product in such form that all the
boss need do is approve or disapprove the completed action. This
sink-or-swim policy does not preclude your making suggestions at the
time the assignment is given out. In fact, it is at that juncture that you
should give guidance and respond to queries and requests for direction.
If you have carefully thought out the assignment, your instructions to
the staff member will be sufficient to finish the product.

Completed staff work frees you from doing the staff's work and
lets you get on with your own job as manager. Responsibility for
development of the recommended completed action rests where that
responsibility belongs – on the staff. After they learn to accept this
responsibility, they are truly in training for those jobs they seek
with more responsibility. In addition, the entire organization is
strengthened.

When you announce that the doctrine of completed staff work will apply to all future work assignments, be sure your instructions make crystal clear what you expect. Of course, the first point to cover is that, from now on, your staff is to submit for your approval only completed work products – no more rough drafts or requests for direction. Naturally, you expect the finished product to be the best possible solution to the assignment. Each staff member is expected to work out for himself the details to reach the completed action for his assignment, no matter how perplexing those details may be. Point out, also, that he should consult with his associates so that proper action can be developed to conclude the assignment, but he should not ask you for guidance, since you want answers, not questions. Neither should he submit long explanations or involved memos, addressed to you, about the assignment. Again, what you want is the completed assignment in final form so that you can approve the action and forward it on its way.

If an employee fails to follow your instructions about completed staff work, return his submission with a note to that effect. Otherwise, if you do more to complete the assignment to your satisfaction, you will be doing the work you've hired someone else to do.

When the staff understands the level of work that you demand from them, they will realize that it's up to them to perform at that level. Meanwhile, you reduce your own inclination to rewrite letters, reports, and memos that should have been adequately completed by your staff before you ever saw them.

With the doctrine of completed staff work in force, everyone, including you, has a better understanding of how you expect to get things done.

You will, of course, need to adapt this 'doctrine' to your professional needs. For instance, the architect of a high-rise building doesn't oversee the laying of every brick or the fitting of every beam, but she does check the pylons after they have all been sunk or the foundation after it has been laid. So, review your subordinates' work at the appropriate stages of completion, but to make the best use of their skills and your time, be sure that everyone understands the need for completed assignments.

Computers

'The real danger is not that computers will begin to think like men, but that men will begin to think like computers.'

Sydney J. Harris

Problem: Edward was not involved with automatic data processing while he was a nonsupervisory employee. Now, as a newly appointed manager, he discovered that the work of the people and machines in the computer unit consumed much of his budget. He sought to determine what he was getting for the money by talking to the people in the computer unit. Their technical mumbo-jumbo language confused him more than it helped him understand their answers to his questions. Since both the computer people and the computers were always busy whenever he visited that area of the office, he hesitated to interrupt them any more than was absolutely necessary.

Approach: Edward probably would benefit from a good short course in 'Computer Training for Managers'. He would learn there that automatic data processing, the function of a computer, is limited only by the imagination of the user of the computer. A computer never thinks independently. A computer's 'brain' is produced and fed by humans. A computer does nothing on its own except malfunction periodically. Although it is a complex machine, remember it is still wholly under human dominance. That's the salient point to keep in mind when you consider the uses of a computer. ·

To benefit from the use of a computer, you don't have to understand how it works. You don't have to be able to converse in computer terminology. You don't have to feel inferior because you don't understand the language of a computer technician. To make a computer work *for* you, you do have to know exactly what you want the computer to do *for* you. Suppose, for instance, your computer now produces a weekly print-out of vacant positions and the name and job title of everyone in your unit. From that listing, the weekly payroll is prepared. When a person resigns, the print-out shows a vacancy so that no paycheck is issued for the position. Although you are personally little concerned with the bare listing of payroll positions, you are concerned about the high rate of employee turnover. You decide to ask that each time a person resigns, the reason for the resignation be placed in the computer. You then ask that this turnover information be sent to you periodically with additional break-downs of information such as sex, age, position, length of service, and organizational unit. With these facts, you can study those parts of the organization requiring special managerial attention (yours) to reduce the high turnover rate. Likewise, you can study those areas of your organization where turnover is not a problem to learn why it is not a problem. As in this example, to make the computer work for you and provide information you can use, you merely submit a request to the computer unit in your own words. The program analysts will convert the request to computer language.

You can overburden yourself with computer reports. If you no longer need or want a piece of computer information, tell the computer people to stop collecting that information for you. Using a computer means controlling a computer. This takes action by you, but first it takes think time so that you get the result that you want when you want it. The possibilities for good things coming out of your computer are plentiful. These possibilities are up to your ingenuity, coupled with your need to know. If your computer people continue to collect and give you information you neither want nor need or you can't get what you do need, work on the situation until your wishes are met. Anything short of that results in the use of the computer being an end in itself rather than a tool for your use in management. Keep in control of the computer or it will control you.

Constructive Tension

'In the battle of existence, Talent is the punch;
Tact is the clever footwork.'

Wilson Mizner

Problem: Barbara knew she had a good staff, one of the best. She was also confident of her managerial ability. The staff and Barbara were sympatico with each other. Nevertheless, she was beginning to experience some serious production problems for no apparent reason. She was soon being quizzed by her boss about the production deficiencies. He wanted a turnaround. She wanted one, too. Barbara became more and more concerned, but her staff evidenced nowhere near her degree of concern. In fact, they acted largely as if nothing were wrong. Barbara began to feel that she was carrying the weight of the staff's production failure entirely on her shoulders.

Approach: Barbara was right, even if she resented the fact: the weight of meeting production goals was on her shoulders. The purpose of an organization is to get something done, and a manager's job is to see that the organization's goals are met. To do this, the manager sets goals and objectives for the persons under her so that her division's portions of the organization's goals are completed. The persons on her staff have been hired to work towards that purpose, whether that purpose is to sell washing machines, to publish books, to manufacture vacuum cleaners – whatever. The manager monitors her staff's progress in meeting the goals. If they are not met, the manager is held to account by her boss. If a manager doesn't produce, the ultimate sanction that can be used against her is dismissal. No manager wants to be fired, so managers are always striving to meet goals.

A manager who is respected, organized, compassionate, and inspirational may clearly tell her staff of the production goals for which they are responsible. That staff may be trained, experienced, and motivated. The office may be a happy place to work with no evident morale problems. But the manager finds that she is not meeting production goals set at the beginning of the year. Nothing has happened to make the goals less attainable, and she can't think of any way to improve production. She has a good organization, but it just isn't producing as anticipated. She's in trouble.

This is where 'constructive tension' comes into play. This is an attitude fostered by the boss to help the staff meet production goals. She demands, with grim conviction, that her staff meet those goals. She expands her demands to include everybody in the office. She reiterates that each person there has but one primary job – that is, to work to meet the production goals. The boss convinces the staff that meeting those goals is what they are paid to do and that their jobs are at stake. She keeps production goals in the forefront of her staff's attention at all times. She never lets the staff or, for that matter, anyone else forget that production is the yardstick by which every person on the staff is measured. Whenever any employee sees the boss or talks to her or even thinks about her, a spectre of production goals is conjured up. When this feeling permeates even the subconscious mind of everyone on the staff, constructive tension has been created. Call it 'mind control' or 'overkill' if you will; in management it's known as 'leadership'. And it gets the job done.

You must not let an attempt to instil constructive tension degenerate into a personal plea to meet production goals. To establish credibility as a leader, you must schedule frequent brief sessions for production accountability. In these sessions with your key staff you will set new minigoals to be achieved by the next session. When one session concludes, set the meeting time for the next one so that you can maintain monitoring continuity. Your staff, in turn, will have to meet with their staffs to assess progress. These face-to-face meetings give you and your staff an opportunity to review developments and to inspire even greater efforts towards achievement of your goals. The responsibility of having to report regularly to the boss serves as an incentive to make sure that each report is a positive one. Any supervisor who finds herself reporting that her production goals are not being met, week after week, realizes that this can go on for just so long. She knows she has to turn her unit's production around so that she can finally start to present good reports. This is how constructive tension works. It motivates the staff.

The word *tension* by itself does not have a good connotation, but if you can develop an attitude of constructive tension in your staff, you'll discover it is just that: constructive, not destructive.

Contractor Accountability

*'The trouble with being tolerant is that people think
you don't understand the problem.'*

Merle L. Meachem

Problem: A sudden unpredicted surge increased the workload of the
division and confronted Stuart with his first major problem in his new
job as head of the division. He knew that he could not quickly hire and
train sufficient staff to handle the increase in work. He wouldn't be
given permission to do that anyway until the permanence of the
increase could be assessed. He could let the backlog mount, but
because funds were available, he decided to contract out the work to an
outside firm. He had never contracted out work before and was surprised at the number of firms available. He made a blind selection of
one firm for a substantial fee. When the first batch of work was
returned, it was a mess, but since no performance standards were
included in the contract, the firm declared the work was satisfactory
and insisted on payment.

Approach: As in Stuart's case, you will find that the need to contract
out work regularly done by your own office may come upon you
suddenly. An army of outside contractors and consultants compete for
such work as automatic data processing, billing, typing, reproduction
overloads, and management studies that could be done within the
home office but that, for any number of reasons, isn't. Demanding that
work done outside the office meet the same standards as you expect for
work done by your own staff is a managerial control that can get
sidetracked. This can happen when the contract is made by someone
not under your supervision, such as your organization's purchasing
department. The beneficiaries of contracts let without the inclusion of
your specific performance standards are the contractors. They end up
with relatively few guidelines other than those that make sure of the
amount of payment they will receive. This is a boon for the contractor,
but the final product, in terms of quality and timing, may be very
unsatisfactory to your office.

Before letting a service contract, the manager for whom the job is
being done needs to list those standards of performance he would
expect for the same job if it were done by his own staff. Incorporating
those standards into the terms of the contract or purchase agreement is
the surest way of holding a contractor responsible for his performance.
If a contractor is unwilling to accept your performance standards,
continue shopping until you find one who is willing to accept them and

is capable of doing the job the way you want it done. If you fail to set standards for work done by outside contractors while insisting on such standards for the same work done internally, you create a dual system of managerial standards. For those within your office, you ask for a certain level of performance, but for those outside you do not demand an equal performance. It's an interesting double standard to try to explain to your staff. In addition, if you do not make your inside-outside standards comparable, you invite the completion of a product that may or may not fulfil your performance standards. In effect, you assure the contractor that you will pay him regardless of the quality of his performance. That's fine for the contractor, but not very fine for you.

Outside performance standards must be in writing and must be clear enough to permit you to withhold payment if those standards, including the delivery time of the product, are not met. For example, if you're contracting out a rush job for, say, something even as simple as a batch of letters to be typed, don't assume the contractor knows exactly what you want. Instead, include specific written job requirements, such as the following on your work order:

> Payment for completed work will be subject to the full satisfaction of the following conditions:

- Type original letters on attached company letterhead.
- Make two carbon copies of each letter (first copy on attached yellow tissue; second copy on attached white tissue).
- Follow exact spacing and styling layout of attached sample.
- Use Pica type.
- Proofread letters and eliminate any mistakes.
- Type addresses on attached company envelopes.
- Proofread typed envelopes and correct any mistakes.
- Attach completed letter and carbons to matching envelope with paper clip. DO NOT FOLD LETTERS.
- Return letters in same order as the attached name and address list.
- Deliver completed order to above address by no later than 72 hours from date and time stamped on this purchase order.

Before you approve payment, be certain that your conditions have been met. Then, and only then, is the payment ripe for release.

Controlling Your Workload

'To do nothing is in every man's power.'
Samuel Johnson

Problem: Ollie wondered how his predecessor planned for the types of work that reached his desk. A month ago, when Ollie became section chief, he was eager to meet the challenges of his new job as they were outlined in the official description. No mention was made of the inconsequential matters that now seemed to consume most of his time. The time left to accomplish those significant matters for which he was supposedly hired was not very great. When he thought about the barrage of telephone calls, in-coming mail, and other requests on his time, he felt like the office junkman.

Approach: Ollie faces the managerial problem of 'if-in-doubt-let-the-boss-handle-it' syndrome. There is no absolute rule declaring that a manager has to receive all the office scraps, big and little. Yet, it can work out that way unless he exercises controls to limit the types of duties that reach him.

It's almost axiomatic that the higher the managerial position, the greater the work volume. That's the way it seems, but it doesn't have to be that way. A manager's life during regular working hours is one of communicating: talking on the phone, delegating work assignments, giving dictation, participating in staff conferences, signing correspondence, and meeting with people. It is a decision-making existence consisting of a chain of listening, talking, and delegating.

If you find yourself unable to manage the volume of work that confronts you, first examine how you spend your working time. When you finish your analysis, make a list of those duties that shouldn't reach you at all because they have so little to do with the meeting of your goals. Routine reports, perhaps important down the line, and other 'nice-to-know' items may consume time you can better spend on more important things. Be brutal and cut down on the time-consumers that reach you. Tell your secretary or whoever routes the items which ones you *don't* want to see.

Examine other time-consumers – meetings, phone calls – that can be delegated without reaching you at all in the first place. In doing this sorting through, issue instructions that you no longer will participate in certain types of meetings or receive certain phone calls. These duties will be handled henceforth by others closer to the problems. Unencumber yourself.

In paring down your workload, be careful not to isolate yourself completely from the office world around you. You'll also have to be sensitive not to farm out so many responsibilities that the office leadership becomes diffused to the point of becoming ineffective. To keep these risks in check, at first reassign only a few items from your cutdown list. Then a few more. Continue until you reach a level that seems right for you. Your aim is to become a better manager, not a less effective one.

After you filter out those chores on which you no longer want to spend time, you may still find your working hours tight, but you will find you have more time for significant matters. To do those 'think time' tasks that require uninterrupted concentration to produce results, look for spots in the day when this is possible. Depending on whether you are a 'morning' person or a 'night' person, consider either coming in early or leaving late to accomplish those tasks. Working at home is, of course, another option, depending on your appetite for that. The method you use depends on what's best for you. Don't be hesitant to engage in trial and-error efforts as you hunt for the right way.

Examining how you spend your working hours is not a one-time venture. Because of the dynamics of a managerial job, you must periodically analyse how you spend your time, so that you can best perform your job. Try to analyse your time at least semi-annually on a fixed schedule in order to force yourself to do it. This way you'll develop the realization that you can control your time and destiny to a greater degree than you first imagined.

Dealing with the Media

'Journalism is literature in a hurry.'
Matthew Arnold

Problem: Mario's secretary startled him with the announcement that 'Some smart-alecky reporter is on the phone and says he absolutely has to talk to you right away'. Mario, who had never been interviewed by a reporter before, asked what the reporter wanted. She said he wouldn't tell her the subject. As Mario tried to collect his wits, he told her to inform the caller that he, Mario, was not available. She replied that the reporter's aggressive manner had already made her admit that Mario was in fact available. Mario was rattled, to say the least, but he picked up the phone. He'd heard about reporters who force people to say things that they later regret, and he feared the worst as he spoke reluctantly into the phone.

Approach: If you have occasion to deal with the media, such an encounter doesn't have to be as frightening as Mario envisaged it. Actually, contacts with the media can be interesting experiences if you have a strategy for responding to their inquiries.

Almost all media contacts come suddenly and end suddenly. Media representatives – newspaper reporters, TV and radio broadcasters – are governed by deadlines for filing their stories. The deadlines are always imminent. That's the way the media operate. This causes what appear to be abrupt – almost rude – demands by media representatives for instant information. But the abruptness results from that ever-present filing deadline. Media competition for the same story adds to the overall forcefulness of the contacts. If a news story of the day is missed, it's missed forever. It is no longer news by tomorrow. Once you understand why media representatives conduct themselves as they do, you can work out a media strategy.

A manager's willingness to respond rapidly to media contacts is essential. If a reporter who contacts you at 11 A.M. has a noon deadline for filing his story, he has to have the story written by then. So, if you want to be responsive, alert your secretary to what media deadlines are all about and ask that such calls be brought to your attention as soon as they are received. Don't forget, too, that secretaries can develop a firm dislike for media representatives because they often aggressively demand to speak to the boss *now*, in order to meet their deadlines.

In talking with the media, be responsive to their questions. If you don't know the answer to one, say so. If a reporter is leaning towards a story angle you don't endorse, tell him so – clearly enough so that he has no doubt about your position. If you feel that the reporter has not allowed you to fully state your position, tell him and then state your position. If a story has two sides, give both sides. By doing so, you can earn a reputation for being a responsible source. The reporters will learn to trust you. Be courteous, honest, and keep to the point. Whatever you say may end up in print or on the air, so if you are in doubt about a fact, don't voice the fact. If you have to check a point before committing yourself, tell that to the reporter. If someone else can answer a question that you cannot, suggest that the reporter contact that person. Above all, keep your wits about you or you may, in the stress of the moment, say things that you'll later wish you hadn't. Never assume anything you say is 'off the record' unless you first ask the reporter if he will accept a comment off the record. The rule is that an informant's request to have his remark be off the record will be honoured only if the request is made before the remark is uttered. Don't expect a reporter to explain the rules of his business to you any more than you expect to explain the rules of yours to him.

When a reporter knows where you're coming from, he'll respect you for it. When *you* know where you're coming from, you'll feel more confident in your ability to deal with the media. You may even enjoy the experience.

Delegating

'That man is great who can use the brains of others to carry out his work.'

Donn Piatt

Problem: When Les was a staff employee, he prided himself on the quality of his work. After becoming a manager, he tried to use these standards to judge the work of those he supervised. Apparently his standards were too high, for he continually returned his staff's completed work with suggestions for improvement. After a while, his staff resigned themselves to the fact that it was impossible to get Les to accept their work on the first submission.

Approach: Poor, poor Les. His unit's production will no doubt suffer until he can accept the notion that his way is not the only way to complete an assignment. To be able to delegate work to others and to be satisfied with the results is an art. Like any art, to become a good delegator takes abundant quantities of skill, practice, and patience. Once acquired, the ability to get things done improves with the level of one's knowledge of what, when, how, and to whom to delegate.

A manager starts the process of getting things done by delegating. A specific assignment can be delegated; a whole area of responsibility can be delegated; correspondence can be delegated; a very narrow activity can be delegated. You can delegate the responsibility for answering a telephone call, for making a business trip, for preparing a budget. About the only activity you cannot delegate is having someone eat your lunch for you.

As a manager you have to delegate almost every work assignment that requires unbroken concentration to complete, even if you would prefer to do the work yourself. To work uninterruptedly on such a project is incompatible with the other demands on a manager's time, unless, of course, you work on the project outside regular office hours. Even then, if you try to do the work in the office itself, you'll have difficulty because of interruptions from others who also are working outside regular office hours. The personal satisfaction of completing a project is something that a manager has to learn to forego. He must delegate the job and accept the fact that it will be completed by others. That is one of the most difficult adjustments for a new manager. With that adjustment, you're on your way to becoming a delegator, not necessarily a good delegator, but a delegator nevertheless. It's then that you can understand that a manager's job is managing the work of others, regardless of whether the manager can do a piece of work better than anyone on his staff.

Early in the process of delegating, it's normal to find yourself dissatisfied with the product returned to you as completed. You won't like the style – it's not your style. You won't like the length of the letter or report – it's not the length you would have made it. You won't like the conclusions of the report – they're not your conclusions. You won't like the tone of a speech prepared for your delivery – it's not your tone. Your growth as a delegator begins when you understand that seldom does a delegated piece of work come back completed exactly the way you'd do it. You'll then comprehend that expecting your staff to be a mirror image of you is neither possible nor desirable.

Everyone 'out there' to whom you delegate work is an individual with ideas and opinions of his own. None is a mirror of you, although each is your representative. Give your staff the latitude of using the diversity of their own individualities to get the job done. Assuming that your staff understands the standards of performance by which they will be judged, constant second guessing or 'improving' their products is a sign of your immaturity as a delegator. Periodically, you will need to restate office objectives and policies to provide the staff with guidance to complete delegated assignments. A statement, too, on the tone you'd like in your letters like – 'use angel words instead of devil words' – may be called for. But once the substantive ground rules are laid, your main function is to monitor to see that those rules are being followed.

Finally, a manager cannot simply delegate a matter and then forget about it. The delegated work has to be completed by a stated deadline. If there are no managerial deadline controls, you are not really delegating. All you're doing is passing work on to others while forgetting your responsibility for following through until the product is completed satisfactorily and on time.

Dictation

Problem: Margo was known as a good writer. That's one of the reasons she was picked to head up the office's newly created 'procedures unit'. As chief of the unit, she still wanted to do some writing, but found her time to do so increasingly limited. As a nonsupervisory employee, she had written her letters and other work in long hand. Since then, she had tried dictating once or twice, but it didn't come out sounding right. Others might be able to save time by dictating, but she was convinced that she could not.

Approach: If Margo's time is as limited as she believes, she should give herself another chance to learn to dictate. Dictating correspondence and other work translates into saving time to do other things. Learning to dictate is like learning to drive a car. It takes time to become skilful. Like anything else, if you work at it, it gets easier. If you work at it persistently enough, you can dictate almost all of your correspondence, memos, and written staff instructions.

Dictation has some unsuspected advantages. For instance, assume you receive a telephone call while you are dictating to your secretary. If your policy is to allow no interruptions while you are dictating, you'll be able to continue until you are finished. The phone call will be answered without your being disturbed. If you are writing out your message in long hand at the time the telephone call is received, you'll probably be interrupted as a matter of course. Then you have to pick up your train of thought after the call or, possibly, be sidetracked altogether. Similarly, if someone drops by to see you while you're dictating, that person usually won't interrupt unless you signify that's your desire. Dictation permits you to start and finish something in one continuous action. With the number of interruptions in a manager's normal work day, that's a luxury a manager learns to savour.

There are other advantages. Dictating an item is much quicker than writing it in long hand; this speed is especially welcome when you need a rough draft fast because you are hot upon an idea. Polishing and revising is easier from the typed copy. If your hand-writing is as poor as mine, you can score a big plus with those who otherwise would have to decipher your scribbling if you eliminate that chore.

Those who say that they can't dictate, that their thoughts come out better in long hand, probably have not given dictation a fair chance or have never even tried to dictate. Dictation does take time before its full benefits can be appreciated. To start developing the skill, try to dictate a memo to record the essence of a phone call. Start your dictation as soon as the call is completed. Since no one expects a file memo about a phone call to be a literary gem, all you need is a clear statement of the discussion and the conclusions that were reached. So ask your secretary to 'bring her book in' and let the story of the phone call roll out from memory or notes. If it's your first try, tell her what you're attempting to accomplish. She'll be sympathetic – which will help.

The first time you dictate expect to be nervous and don't expect too much of the product. As you gain proficiency, your confidence will grow so that you will widen the range of situations in which you use dictation.

When you are out of the office or when your secretary is not available, use one of the many small dictation recording devices that are on the market. You might even decide to use a mechanical device for all dictation rather than dictating directly to a secretary. Some people like to dictate to a secretary whenever possible, but that's a personal preference.

Discussion Groups

*'The most immutable barrier in nature is between
one man's thoughts and another's.'*

William James

Problem: Von's unit was under pressure to raise production. The
spirited young professional staff working for him responded mar-
vellously. Their production rose quickly and dramatically. With such a
rapid production increase, however, a bottleneck developed in the
completion of the work by the nonprofessional staff. The more the
professionals pushed, the more the nonprofessionals felt picked on and
unappreciated. Nonprofessional staff turnover almost kept pace with
the production leaps of the professionals. Each side blamed the other
openly for the situation.

Approach: In the last few years, 'employee rap sessions' (discussion
groups) have sprung up in offices and shops around the United States.
Starting one of these programmes might help Von. Instead of just a
chat session at the coffee break, some office discussion groups evolve
into a discussion of topics at times announced well in advance to encourage good attendance. The women's liberation and the civil rights
movements inspired these sessions, although topics have expanded
beyond those movements. At the sessions, employees listen to others'
views, organize programmes to overcome real or suspected injustices,
and develop arguments to influence an organization's policies.

When these sessions got underway in earnest in my office, I decided,
as manager, to organize my own discussion groups. So I invited all
employees to my office for an open discussion on things they wanted to
complain about to me or to anyone present. The session was prompted
by signs from the secretarial and clerical staff that they thought they
were poorly treated by the professional staff. This attitude was
reflected in the high turnover rate in their ranks. This problem had
occurred before during my career, but I had never before attempted
to find the solution by scheduling open discussions with those
affected.

The first session resulted in a thorough 'let-it-all-hang-out' discussion and airing of the problems on both sides. This and followup
sessions resulted in immediate action to overcome the simpler complaints. Lighting was improved in the clerical and secretarial area, and
training was provided for complicated office equipment. Solutions to
more involved problems took longer. From a secretarial and clerical
viewpoint, the best part of the rap sessions was seeing management

take the risk to open itself up to criticism and then to do something about that criticism. Somebody cared after all.

I started a second type of discussion group at about the same time. In these I included only my top staff. We convened approximately once a month. Before each one, I invited suggestions for possible topics. Then, on a consensus basis, one topic was discussed at each session. Needed followup actions were summarized at the end of each one. The topics included equal opportunities, staff training, promotional opportunities, office space, and other subjects that make up the concerns of supervisory staff. For some sessions, such as those on staff training, I invited specialists from outside the organization in order to obtain their views and possible involvement in followup actions.

The value of a discussion group begun by management lies not in just opening up the organization to criticism. The value lies in the strengthening of the organization if management does something to improve the items criticized. It's also recognized as a progressive move when management shows a willingness to listen and learn.

Easy Does It

'It is a luxury to be understood.'
Ralph Waldo Emerson

Problem: Everyone knew that Chris had a driving ambition to succeed, no matter what. He came to work early and he left late. He was all business and expected the same of his staff. He became upset whenever he came upon a group of his employees who were laughing or gossiping. He regarded this as a waste of time. He believed that the discussion of any activity other than the work of the office was frivolous nonsense, since nothing was as important as achieving the goals of the office.

Approach: Chris probably saw no truth in the old adage that you can catch more flies with honey than with vinegar. I once had a boss like Chris. He came to work each morning and spoke to no one as he marched by desk after desk to reach his own cubicle. He developed a reputation as a lone workhorse who did not care about his staff. This reputation resulted in a staff that did not work at all well for him. Partly because of his aloofness, the staff didn't really want to work for him. My boss displayed other peculiar traits that compounded the problems of the office, but his habit of ignoring everyone upon his arrival each morning set a tone of isolation from the staff that stretched throughout the day.

To greet co-workers cheerfully as you begin the day will not guarantee that your day will be a success. Far from it. However, such a greeting does start each day off on a positive note instead of a negative one. To convince the staff of your sincerity, you have to communicate a positive attitude to them all day long. Office communication is not just a matter of writing memos. Chances are excellent that the aims of those memos will not be met unless they are part of an overall communications effort. No need to gush, but make sure the communication process begins with the morning greeting and continues in one form or another through the working day.

A good working atmosphere requires that communications expand to include more than the specific work goals of the office. To set an aura of mutual good will and trust, take the time to exchange pleasantries and exhibit an interest in events outside the office. The staff gains a view of you, the boss, as a whole person, and you appreciate them more, too. Gone is any hint that the staff is a bunch of robots with no purpose in life outside the purpose of the office. To establish this type of office communication helps to control any personal antipathy with which the staff may be inclined to regard you.

The list of normal office irritations for employees is long enough without the addition of personal dislike. The development of mutual good feelings between staff and boss won't make a poor boss or a poor staff a winner, but it does help create an environment for working together. There is no sure-fire formula, but when you hit upon a good one, you'll know it. In the meantime, extend yourself to your staff. Be open with them. Let them receive you as you receive them. Get to know each other better. Nurture your office relationships on a continuing basis. Permit the staff to want to do things for you – and you for them.

Equal Opportunities Personnel Practices

'If it wasn't for Abe [Lincoln], I'd still be on the open market.'

Dick Gregory

Problem: When Alex was appointed to head the division, his boss told him to improve the division's record for hiring and promoting ethnic and other minority group employees. This was Alex's top priority. As soon as he reported to his new job, he told his staff about the boss's views on minorities and endorsed them as his own. He emphasized that he expected results. He then became immersed in other problems of his division. The minority situation didn't improve, so Alex again told his staff that he expected them to hire and to promote qualified minority employees. Still nothing happened.

Approach: When Alex complained of lack of action on his positive action directives, he probably heard his people say, 'I can't find qualified minority people.' That's a common lament of those charged with recruiting blacks, disabled people, women, and other minorities. In response to such a cry, a manager must first analyse the type of minority programme his organization has. Are minority persons actively sought? If not, your minority recruiting programme cannot compete with those of companies who are active in this regard. Your programme will also lack the commitment to go those extra steps to recruit minority workers.

There are no secret methods for establishing and maintaining an effective minority recruitment programme. The prime ingredients for success are the same as for other managerial responsibilities – a plan, commitment, accountability, follow-through, rewards, and sanctions. The difficulty in setting up a minority recruitment programme is the long tradition of not hiring minorities for any good jobs, coupled with outright prejudice. Overcoming these obstacles requires an exceptional degree of managerial persistence. You must recognize the difficulties because the success of the programme depends upon staying with it over the long haul.

A manager has to impress upon his staff that he is committed to hiring minorities for legal, moral, and common sense reasons. He lets his staff know that he also expects them to commit themselves not only to hiring minorities, but to training and promoting them as well. He impresses on his staff that this policy is a part of their jobs and will remain an important element in judging their individual job effectiveness.

As a followup to such stated commitment, require each of your supervisors to submit an action plan. Ask for updated plans at intervals. The original plan must be balanced – covering a period short enough so that specific actions are scheduled, but also long enough so that realistic goals are outlined. Each supervisor determines what has to be done to make his plan work. The better parts of each plan can ultimately be combined in a model that can be followed by all supervisors under your direction.

Inform your staff members that their performance evaluations will include a major line item on this area of responsibility, so they realize that this function is part of their jobs. With such accountability, supervisors will be inclined to watch each other's progress and to compare notes on the more effective methods. When this stage is reached, progress is emerging. Real progress, though, will be evident when minorities are on the payroll in responsible positions.

The gratifying part of this effort occurs when a minority employee starts blossoming, and you realize how that process was locked out of your organization in the past through lack of an equal opportunities programme.

Filing Systems

'To solve a problem it is necessary to think. It is necessary to think even to decide what facts to collect.'

Robert Maynard Hutchins

Problem: During the first three weeks Zelda held the position of section manager, she received two separate requests for new filing cabinets. She wondered wryly when she would get the next request. In an office bulging with filing cabinets, she had already discovered that it was difficult to retrieve anything from the files on short notice. And sometimes on long notice. Whenever anything was located, it was presented to her with triumph tinged with surprise. When she decided one day to look for a document in the files herself, her secretary chuckled and said, 'Good luck!' Zelda failed to see humour in the situation.

Approach: Since Zelda's mettle is aroused, she may try to remedy the problem of her bottomless-pit files. Managers generally have little to do with the office filing system until it gets chaotic. When a new office or a new activity begins, a filing system is usually started haphazardly and maintained by the clerical staff. When the system gets hopelessly overburdened, and in my career I've seen more than one such disaster, management is compelled to take an active role to unsnarl the system.

To rate the quality of your filing system, determine how long it takes to retrieve a file. That's a first priority. Then find out how long a file is kept before being discarded or retired to an inactive status.

Once these questions are answered, put forth a second set of questions. Why is a particular piece of paper saved at all? Why can't it be retrieved faster? If there is a disposal and retirement schedule, how can the schedule be improved? These are good starters for getting some managerial understanding of the filing system. When a manager has answers to these questions, she can then decide on the best filing procedure for her organization.

Most filing systems are based on the conservative notion that everything produced in, or received by, the office must be saved because it will be needed in the future. However, I've found that most items are never referred to again. Until the manager takes the time – and courage – to redesign the office filing system and authorize destruction, or at least retirement, of much of the material, her files will continue to bulge, no matter how good the system may be.

One office manager I met handled this battle of the bulge by keeping all file copies in chronological order and retaining them for one year. If no one needed them by the end of that year, he destroyed the material. Whatever file was referred to during the first year after it had been created was retained for a year following the date of reference to it. This manager had no bulging file cabinets and insisted that he had seldom been hampered by his rather daring system of file disposal.

While you may not want to follow such an extreme example, you still would like to set up an ideal system. That is the one in which only those items are kept that will ever be needed again. This would cut filing time, simplify retrieval, and reduce cabinet cost and space. So try to design your system to approach the ideal, but be prepared to risk destroying some items you may need unexpectedly at some future time. As long as you're not violating the law, this risk is worth taking.

Flexible Working Hours

'Time is a circus always packing up and moving away.'
                                                    Ben Hecht

Problem: When the central personnel office polled Lee's staff about changing their working hours to a flexible schedule more convenient to each of them, Lee predicted the affirmative vote that resulted. But he couldn't understand why the personnel office would consider such a proposal in view of the managerial problems that would ensue. He had enough problems without another big headache being tossed in his lap. His lack of enthusiasm for flexible working hours was well known to his staff, but they endorsed the change anyway.

Approach: Lee might have investigated the experiences of organizations using flexible working hours before condemning the system. I felt much as he did when flexi-time was proposed for my office. The traditional fixed office hours for everyone were so set in my mind that when the proposal was made to allow employees to pick their own starting and leaving times, within a certain block of hours, I'll have to admit I was apprehensive. Employees were asked to select a starting time no earlier than 6:30 A.M. and a leaving time of no earlier than 3:00 P.M., as long as each employee put in a full eight and one-half hours a day, including lunch time. The regular working hours for those not wanting to change would remain in effect. The purpose of allowing flexible working hours was to permit greater accommodation in the personal lives of employees. In theory, to permit such an accommodation would benefit the office because the employees would be more satisfied.

Management concerns were: Who would supervise an employee arriving for work at 6:30 in the morning? Would these early birds actually work? If a secretary wanted to set her leaving time at 3:00, but her boss didn't leave until 5:00, should her boss go along with her schedule? If a staff member picked early departure time, would this wipe out late-day staff meetings because of a missing staff member?

As it turned out, relatively few employees elected to change their normal working hours. But they liked to have the option to do so. Whether they changed their working hours or not, the staff felt more in control of their destinies. It took time for supervisors to adjust to the new schedules, but this was a minor problem.

This type of innovation, which appears radical on its face, is a positive managerial move. To give something so small to your staff without asking for anything tangible in return will never hurt you as a manager. So instead of merely reacting to the concept of flexible working hours, analyse the possible results of adopting such a proposal. Decide whether this is a change you wish to incorporate into your office routine. If you're not fully convinced that it will work in your office but see it working elsewhere, give yourself a chance to evaluate the system first-hand by installing it on a 90-day trial basis. At the end of that period, you ought to know for sure one way or the other.

Following Through

*'My interest is in the future because I am going to
spend the rest of my life there.'*

Charles F. Kettering

Problem: One of the first discoveries Stanley made as a manager was
that his staff frequently did not meet deadlines. Before Stanley became
a manager, he had seldom failed to meet an assigned deadline, so he had
difficulty understanding his staff's dereliction of duty. When he
assigned work to the staff, he imposed individual deadlines for completion of the work. When a deadline was missed, only infrequently did
the staff member come forward to tell Stanley the reason for the failure
or when the work would be completed.

Approach: Like Stanley, you can spend much time conceiving a plan
of action and then ask that it be implemented only to see little or no
compliance with your request. The same may go for your most routine
directive with a deadline whether you ask for a followup action on a
telephone inquiry or for the preparation of a letter.

It sometimes appears as if no one pays attention to anything you say.
This is a common complaint of managers. Nothing timely will happen
unless you have a procedure for following through on your action
requests. Because you as a boss ask for something to be done is no
guarantee that it will be done. A boss has to appreciate this management fact. But understanding is only the beginning. You must do
something to make sure that your people do heed your requests. This is
called follow through.

One method of following through on work assignments is to set up a
tickler file that shows the items due for completion on any given day. If
the item will not be completed on time, place the responsibility for
telling you so, with reasons, on the person to whom you assigned the
project. Insist that he inform you before the deadline so that catch-up
steps can be considered. When it's clear that a deadline will be missed,
always set a new deadline. Never leave the due date open ended. This
new deadline date goes into your tickler date file for follow up. The
person responsible for completion of each assignment knows that you
will keep track of the due date. Each of them knows those sanctions
you have at your command to penalize those who miss deadlines.

The establishment of a tickler date file, of course, will not solve the
problem of employee inaction and delinquency. If the initial deadline
can be missed, so can the next one. Your job is to analyse the reasons for
failure to meet due dates so that action can be taken to correct the

problem. For instance, your analysis may reveal that the problem is a lack of communication, or that the employee responsible for the late assignment has too much other work. Once you uncover what's wrong, you can start to solve the problem. A manager's follow-through habit is prerequisite to success. Without this unglamorous day-in and day-out grinding away at polishing your system for getting things to move, they will not move the way you'd like. Even with the best system of follow through, and with the most dogged supervisory determination, there will still be occasional missed deadlines. Nevertheless, without a good follow-through system, expect no more than a mediocre deadline-meeting operation. Your staff, in a very normal behaviour pattern, will be lax on meeting deadlines if you do not convince them otherwise.

Getting Things Off Your Chest

*'Remember, no one can make you feel
inferior without your consent.'*
Eleanor Roosevelt

Problem: Jim knew that he had a reputation among his employees for being 'soft'. As a new boss, he started out wanting to be known as a 'nice guy'. To preserve this nice-guy image, he seldom called anyone to task for fear of being labelled 'mean'. When some of Jim's staff realized that they could do anything they wanted to do without fear of sanctions, they grew careless, and production slipped. Jim could see things getting worse and worse, but he continued to hide his aggravation rather than speak out because he didn't want anyone to dislike him.

Approach: If you are a 'nice guy', you probably have some of Jim's problems. Suppose your secretary arrives ten minutes late for work each day. Or suppose your chief assistant wants you to review once again a rough draft of a memo she's preparing for your signature. Or suppose one of your unit chiefs permits her people to take excessively long coffee breaks and takes no action to stop the practice.

What to do? None of these habits makes the office fall apart, but each of them bothers you. And bothers you. And bothers you. You spend part of each day fuming about the abuses. To resolve the problems, you have to face the fact that once a pattern of abuse sets in, it will not improve unless you, as the boss, do something about it. You may, of course, still elect to go on being bothered and let things get even worse, but there are ways to alter these abuses.

The direct approach – as hard as it may be to use the first time – has proved to be the best approach for me. I first used this approach when one day I decided to stop fuming to myself and try instead to correct my secretary's habitual tardiness. I bit my lip, took a deep breath, and wondered how to bring up the subject. I finally called her into my office, shut the door, and asked why she was late to work each morning. Her answer was surprising: 'I didn't realize it made any difference. Nobody ever said anything about it before.' And she began coming in on time.

Fortunately for me, this occurred early in my managerial career. From this and subsequent problems I learned that the direct approach places the responsibility for corrective action upon those creating the problem. Attacking the problem directly also eliminates that nagging feeling that you ought to do something about a bad situation. You may not always solve your problem as easily as I corrected my secretary's tardiness, but you will feel better for having voiced your concern.

Before I adopted the direct approach, I would have solved the problem of my secretary's tardiness by issuing a general staff memorandum, without identifying anyone, on the subject of reporting to work on time. The results of such indirect approaches compared poorly with the effectiveness of the direct approach.

Few problems are as easily solved as my secretary's tardiness, but until you meet the problem directly, you are not even seeking the solution. If you meet the problem head on, you communicate some managerial characteristics about yourself to your staff: you concern yourself with office inequities; you concern yourself about supervisors doing their jobs; you concern yourself about root causes of problems; you concern yourself about solutions. You are a concerned manager! Believe it or not, you'll find your staff appreciates your directness in most instances. In the direct approach, it's important to keep your balance by seeking out the reasons for an abuse before jumping in head first to demand the solution. As an example, excessive coffee breaks may mean a lack of work rather than what appears to be a neglect of work. You can take it from there.

Gripers

*'As I grow older, I pay less attention to what men say.
I just watch what they do.'*

Andrew Carnegie

Problem: Everyone complains sometimes, but Howard carried his complaints to preposterous lengths. He hardly ever opened his mouth except to berate someone or something. The office staff went into hiding whenever he was in their vicinity. No one wanted to be cornered by him and listen to his whining. The staff would go to such extremes as to feign a telephone call to avoid listening to Howard's diatribe. Even Charlie, the new section manager, found himself adopting such tactics. Regardless, Howard was very persistent and continued to mouth off to Charlie and everyone else with complaint after complaint.

Approach: Howard is an example of the employee who seems to spend his entire working career complaining. Nothing is ever right. Whatever is done is wrong. Wrong. Wrong. Wrong. When you detect such an employee heading your way, the natural reaction is to go the other way. He's so predictable, so negative, so destructive, so demoralizing, and so plain boring that you don't want anything to do with him. Even though you're the boss, you're no different in this respect from everyone else.

But, for a manager, there is another approach. The next time you're confronted by such an employee, ask him to come into your office. Have him sit down and tell you his complaint of the moment in detail. Ask him how he would solve the situation if he had the authority. Hear him out. Then ask him to prepare a written analysis of the complaint, a solution or solutions, and the benefits he expects will result from solving the problem. Set a firm date for submission of his written report. If the employee is one who does not normally report directly to you, tell him that you will discuss the submission with his supervisor for a possible adjustment in the deadline, so the complainant's regular work won't suffer. Also ask him to route the completed report to you through his supervisor. There is a good possibility that the employee will resist preparing the requested report. If he decides not to prepare the report, go along with him the first time, but explain that if he complains to you again, you will expect to receive such analysis in writing.

You may surprise and alarm him at the same time. The surprise will come from the novelty of anyone wanting to see a detailed analysis of his complaint. The alarm will come from being asked to put up or shut up.

It's not too hazardous to predict that he'll avoid his chronic complaining to you in the future once he's aware of your ground rules. In the event he elects to submit a report, you can make a decision on his analysis. To make a decision is something you do many times a day anyway. It's even possible that his written analysis might be worthwhile. And a manager needs all the help he can get in solving problems, no matter how unpleasant the wrappings around the solutions.

Handling Pressure

'Anything for a quiet life; as the man said when he took the situation at the lighthouse.'

Charles Dickens

Problem: Jodie liked the salary she received for managing. She also like the prestige, power, and perquisites that went with the job. But, overall, she didn't like the job. Every managerial job she had ever had was so demanding, the problems so unrelenting, that she hated the idea of spending the rest of her working life as a manager. No matter how many managerial problems she solved, there were always more. If only she could put a moratorium on new managerial problems, her life would be so much easier.

Approach: Any new manager soon realizes that life consists of a constant stream of paperwork, deadlines, personnel problems, production problems, budget problems, telephone calls, and meetings, all of which require decisions, decisions, decisions. This realization can make a manager like Jodie wonder whether this is a working life worth continuing.

For most managers, the dream of breaking loose from managerial bonds is a fantasy. Nice escapism, but fantasy still. Family responsibilities, the lack of financial resources, and the absence of a plan for independence result in hopelessness for shedding the managerial life with its dissatisfactions. The fantasy of escape causes a conviction that the problems can be left behind for some unknown dreamland.

In today's difficult managerial world, such discontent, uncertainty, and restlessness are not unusual. After a person rises to a managerial position, she finds her dream of being the boss often turns out to be better than the job itself. Acceptance of the reality that to be a manager means a life of problem-solving is basic to finding contentment as a manager. No matter how well a manager performs, she will always be faced with problems. That's the nature of a manager's job. There is no promised land in which, through hard work, ingenuity, understanding, and patience, a manager reaches a state of tranquillity free of managerial problems. To work towards a tranquil state is one thing. To believe you can achieve such a state is another. A manager's satisfactions come through getting others to accomplish the goals of the organization.

Once a manager realizes that her life is pressure filled and consists of doses of turmoil, regardless of her achievements, she enters a stage of maturity. The sooner she reaches this stage, the better. To understand the demands of her life as a manager, she must come to terms with her job instead of fighting those demands. A manager also has to understand that it takes all the ability she has to stay on top of the problems she faces. To adopt this approach creates a release valve because she consciously recognizes that managerial pressures are part of her job. Until a manager accepts this job outlook, life will be more difficult than necessary both for herself and for those she manages. As Harry Truman was fond of saying, 'If you can't stand the heat, get out of the kitchen'.

If you want to stay in the 'kitchen', approach your next managerial problem as a challenge. Calmly say to yourself, 'I accept this challenge, and I shall come up with the best solution I can, no more, no less.' If necessary, stand back and imagine what you would advise someone else in your position to do. Deliberately try this challenge approach continuously until it becomes second nature. Like me, your only regret will probably be that you didn't try it sooner.

Hiring the Best

'Only a mediocre person is always at his best.'
Somerset Maugham

Problem: Several months after Bruce became unit manager, his deputy resigned to take a more responsible position. When Bruce sought a replacement, three candidates applied. One was outstanding. The other two barely qualified. Bruce was still feeling his way, but he already knew he would have trouble meeting the demands of his job in several areas in which the outstanding candidate shone. Bruce felt threatened by these abilities of the best candidate and found himself leaning towards selecting one of the two mediocre candidates.

Approach: Bruce has historic support for seriously considering selection of a less than outstanding candidate. Some years ago, during US Senate confirmation hearings concerning a Supreme Court nominee, a storm of protest erupted when one of the senators defended the alleged mediocrity of the nominee. The media had a field day with the notion that a US senator not only tolerated mediocrity in a candidate to sit on our highest court, but, in fact, encouraged that quality. He was quoted in the press as stating that mediocrity needed representation.

Although mediocrity had its defenders, the idea of encouraging it was decried across the country. Until this mediocrity incident erupted, you might have thought that no mediocre person had ever been employed deliberately for any job of consequence. The fact is that many mediocre persons are intentionally employed every day. Sometimes this happens because no one else is available at the time of hiring. Other times, one is hired, even though better qualified people are available, because that's the type of individual the person doing the hiring wants. Some bosses, such as Bruce, knowingly employ mediocre people due to their own fears that they may be shown up by a superior employee. Ultimately, far from protecting himself, such an insecure boss plants the seeds of his own destruction by building and maintaining an organization that is inherently less than it need be.

Employing the very best people is the soundest insurance that any manager, even an insecure one, can obtain for himself and his organization. A manager is judged on his performance. His performance depends on the performances of his staff. If his staff is incapable of high-level performance, the poor quality of the manager's performance is predestined. Yet, some managers, capable enough in other respects, believe that they personally will look better if their staffs are inadequate. For a manager to follow this route connotes a failure to understand that a manager survives only by working through others. A manager who is mediocre in many respects himself can overcome the appearance of mediocrity by acquiring an outstanding staff. Casey Stengel, a so-so baseball manager before managing the New York Yankees during their dominance in the 1940s and 1950s, understood this principle fully when, after another championship season, he proclaimed, 'I couldn't have done it without the players.'

Holiday Scheduling

'The end of labour is to gain leisure.'
Aristotle

Problem: Henry became head of the division in May, just before the beginning of the summer holiday period. He knew he needed all the staff support he could garner in his first few months on the job in order to get over the hump. Much to his dismay, three of the five unit chiefs who reported to him began their annual summer holidays on the same day in June. Another unit chief got sick the following week, and the last one was away at a training seminar. Henry felt lost. He struggled with division problems without the help of his seasoned unit chiefs. After this experience he vowed that never again would he be stranded by all of his top staff at the same time.

Approach: Good for Henry! Without proper planning the leadership continuity of an organization can fall apart during the summer holiday period. Unless controls are established, all of your top managers may be gone from the office at the same time, as Henry found out.

The controls don't have to be elaborate. For example, assume you have several supervisory chiefs reporting directly to you. Mark your calendar so that in late winter you remind yourself to circulate a vacation scheduling sheet to these supervisors.

To maintain leadership strength and continuity during the summer, indicate to your unit chiefs that you do not want more than a specified number of them to be off at one time. In the event of a conflict, ask the chiefs to resolve it among themselves before submitting the schedule to you. Suggest, also, that they circulate similar schedules to their own staff members along with the ground rules they believe are needed to maintain operations.

This procedure prevents wholesale gaps in your top leadership structure and spaces out the staff's summer holiday schedule. It also results in minimal top-side interference with one of the most cherished rewards for working. If necessary, similar controls should be invoked for other heavy holiday periods.

In-Tray Control

*'It is not enough to be busy . . . the question is:
What are we busy about?'*
                                        Henry David Thoreau

Problem: After Lou was promoted to his first managerial job as section chief, no one gave him any instructions on how to cope with the stream of demands on his time. As a staff member of the section, he had never suffered for lack of work, but his first few weeks as chief made him wonder whether he would be able to handle the volume of work on his new job. One of the most perplexing parts was trying to manage his in-tray, into which people funnelled papers all day long. As he fell behind the demands of his in-tray, other work seemed to pile up correspondingly.

Approach: As Lou quickly found out, when you rise from the ranks to manager, you learn that the volume of work to be done can expand to a depressing level. To keep things in motion, the skill of a juggler is required. This is especially true in regard to that monster known as the 'in-tray', the repository of all types of demands on your time. When you were a staff employee with no supervisory responsibilities, you could fall behind in the work in your in-tray with relatively little effect on others. When you fall behind as a manager, there's a chain reaction. The reason is that a manager's job is to manage others so that those others get the job done. If, as a manager, you fail to stay up on the work piled in your in-tray, much of which work needs to be delegated by you, others on your staff are held back from their work.

Instead of being discouraged by the in-tray pile-up, develop a system that keeps the in-tray under control. It can be done. To stay on top of your in-tray deposits, you need managerial working habits that instantly categorize the relative importance of items that lodge there. Everything is not equally important simply because it is under your jurisdiction – or because it is sitting in your in-tray awaiting disposition.

Establish a ranking system for your work in the order of importance to the goals of your organization. The higher the ranking, the sooner you work on that item. For example, assume your secretary feeds your in-tray several times a day. It's your job to determine the relative importance of this material and then act on the items as ranked. Scan your in-tray material as quickly as possible after it arrives and classify the material rapidly into the following categories:

1. urgent, needs immediate attention.
2. important, but not urgent.
3. urgent, important, or routine items requiring your signature.
4. 'need-to-know' reports and memorandums.
5. 'nice-to-know' reports and memorandums.
6. misrouted stuff that should never have reached you in the first place.

Once each in-tray item is placed into one or another of the six piles, you have established a work priority. Start with pile no 1, the urgent pile, and begin to make disposition of it. Take some action on each item. Do not let the material simply sit in unattended piles. By the time you reach piles 4 and 5, you'll probably mark some of them for a later, more thorough reading. There's nothing wrong with retaining this material and postponing your action on it, since it is neither urgent nor so important as to require immediate completion. The stuff in the last pile that never should have reached you in the first place is a special problem. The items can either be discarded, returned to your secretary for proper routing, or returned to her with a note not to route this type of material to you in the future.

If one of your problems is an in-tray pile-up caused by your secretary feeding the box too infrequently or at the wrong times, such as just before lunch or near quitting time, have her change to times more convenient for you. She can also flag those items she considers urgent by red-tagging them and placing them on the top of your in-tray pile.

Mastery of the in-tray determines how you keep the flow of much of the incoming and outgoing work moving in your office. Undue delay in making individual decisions on what to do with the contents of your in-tray or concentrating your time on the wrong items particularly complicates your job because your staff will eventually waste your time and theirs on inquiries on the status of in-tray items they have sent to you for action. Judging the importance of each in-tray item and promptly disposing of it prevents this problem from arising and, instead, earns you the reputation of being decisive. So stop worrying about in-tray material swamping you and attack it with an item-by-item priority system to place yourself in control.

Integrity

'This above all: To thine own self be true,
And it must follow, as the night the day,
Thou canst not then be false to any man.'
William Shakespeare

Problem: After Doug had been a manager for a while, he began to receive requests for evaluations of employees of his who were seeking other jobs. Doug's attitude made it difficult for him to respond to such inquiries. He didn't want to lose good employees to another organization. But it would be fine with him to lose those employees whom he considered to be below par or troublesome. Although he was unaware of any instance where a boss attempted to hold back a good employee by giving a 'bad' reference, it was common knowledge that undesirable employees were often given good references to get rid of them. He was tempted, even encouraged by fellow managers, to untruthfully praise a poor employee when questioned by a prospective employer.

Approach: If Doug asked my advice, I would suggest he follow the old bromide, 'honesty is the best policy'. I once inherited an administrative assistant who was a source of great consternation to everyone in the office. His job required him to submit financial reports by a specific date each month. It was nip and tuck whether he would be 'healthy' enough to report for work on those crucial days during which the information for his reports had to be gathered, consolidated, and submitted. As often as not, he would call in sick in the morning and offer a promise to come in 'later'. Usually 'later' never came. I tried everything I could think of to motivate him to improve his job performance, but it became more and more evident that his poor attendance was rooted in deep emotional problems. My fairly diplomatic suggestions that he seek professional help were rejected angrily. Because of the importance of his position and the effect his job performance was having on his associates, I had to consider removing him from the job. This is always a distasteful task. However, I was convinced it was the only way out in this case.

With the knowledge that removal proceedings were under consideration, he began to make job inquiries elsewhere. I held out little hope that his search would be successful until I received a telephone call from another employer requesting a reference on my administrative assistant. The caller said he was seriously interested in hiring my employee and asked for my opinion of the employee's performance. Joy of joys! This was a call I never expected, but I couldn't bring myself to be untruthful about the employee. Something prevented me from trying to palm this poor employee off on someone else. My policy has always been to give a straightforward rundown on any reference checks, as hard as that might be to do in an instance such as this. I blinked, swallowed hard, and told the truth. I told the caller that the employee had difficulty working under pressure, had chronic problems with tardiness and absences, and had trouble meeting deadlines. I did stress his chief strength, which was great accuracy with figures. Once you received a report from him, you knew it was correct.

After I finished, I began to smile at the caller's response. He said that the employee's traits sounded just fine to him. He was trying to fill a job that had no real pressure and did not require high reliability. (I suppose the last person in the job had left because of lack of sufficient things to do.) Anyway, my problem employee got the job, and presto, a giant-sized problem disappeared from my office.

The moral of this story is not that virtue triumphs and everybody lives happily ever after. The point is that if you do play the game straight, along the way you may find some rewarding experiences. But, more important, with your integrity intact, you'll sleep better at night and so will those with whom you do business.

Interviewing Job Seekers

*'The closest to perfection a person ever comes is
when he fills out a job application form.'*
Stanley J. Randall

Problem: When a resignation occurred in the staff in Ethel's unit, she
dreaded the prospect of interviewing and selecting a person to fill the
resulting vacancy. The job interviews mostly came when Ethel was
deeply involved in an important project. Her enthusiasm for such an
interview was also dampened because she knew that she was not a good
interviewer. When an interview was finished, she usually based her
judgment on a gut reaction and then moved on to interview the next
candidate. She tried to complete the whole process rapidly so she could
get back to her other work.

Approach: If you see yourself reflected in this picture of Ethel, it may
be that you have not faced up to what the task of job interviewing
entails. Interviewing a job applicant requires preparation on the part of
the interviewer as well as the applicant. Because the power to hire rests
with the interviewer, she may feel secure in entering the job interview
cold. After all, what has she got to lose? That attitude is a mistake.

To see why it is a mistake, look at the job interview from the
applicant's standpoint. Chances are that he has prepared himself for the
interview. He assessed his experience, his strengths, and his weaknesses, so that he can put his best foot forward, emphasize his strengths
and downplay his weaknesses. To meet the applicant on even terms,
the interviewer needs to be at least as well prepared. How else can she
select the best applicant for the job? As an interviewer, you need all the
competence you can muster because employee selection constitutes a
high-risk venture no matter how good you may be as an interviewer.
Study your turnover rate if you need to be convinced. Think of some of
the mistakes you've hired. Think of some of the jewels you've hired.
When you look back, could a better job of interviewing and screening
have eliminated any of the mistakes?

Although each job interviewer has to develop a style with which he is
at ease, going into an interview unprepared won't do it. A method I've
used over the years is to regard the interview as the second part of a
three-part hiring process. The first part is your preparation for the
interview. Then there is the interview itself, and last is your post-
interview follow-up.

Each job has individual requirements. These are the basic skills
required to perform the job. Make a list of those skills as part of your

preparation for the interview. Then add to the list those personal traits, such as 'penchant for details', 'must be a self-starter', or 'ability to write well', that you consider essential to the job. Only after you've finished this analysis of the job is it time to review the job applications. As you review each written application, compare the application with your checklist. You can thus make a preliminary evaluation of each applicant's skills and personal traits before the interview itself. You can flesh-out the list by adding areas of inquiry suggested by information on the applications.

Now the time for the interview arrives. First off, see that distractions are kept to a minimum. Close the door to your office. Then get the applicant to talk by asking him to summarise his background. Keep the interview conversational by asking questions to bring out responses to items on your checklist. Get the applicant to give you his evaluation of his best and worst points. I make a point of asking 'What do you like to do most?' and 'What do you like to do least?' The answers can be enlightening. If someone tells you outright that he doesn't like details and 'penchant for details' is a must on your list, chalk up one for yourself. If an applicant says he has no weak points, well, watch out. I've interviewed people who have said this probably because no one had ever asked them before to admit their weak points.

Since a job applicant applies for a specific job, ask him for his understanding of the job's responsibilities and requirements. Do this before you give him your rundown on the job. You may be surprised at how different his version of the job is from yours.

Right after the job interview, write down your impressions of the candidate's qualifications. Give an overall rating of poor, fair, good, or outstanding. If you think the applicant is worth considering further, try checking out his references. By the very nature of references, you'll get positive responses, but see what happens when you ask about a few of the items on your checklist. Ask the person to suggest others whom you might contact to learn more about the applicant. Since these persons may not have an axe to grind, they may furnish you with some valuable insights about your prospective employee. Write a summary of each post-interview follow-up.

Once the applicant is on the payroll, you'll soon know the results of your efforts. If the applicant doesn't turn out to be all that you judged at the time of hiring, analyse how you could have done better during the screening process. Add what you learn from this self-evaluation to your interviewing process the next time around as you sharpen your interviewing skills.

Knowing Your Job

*'Knowledge is the only instrument of production
that is not subject to diminishing returns.'*
                                        J. M. Clark

Problem: When Dan was picked to head his division, with him came
his reputation as the best engineer the division ever had. His ability to
solve complex problems and to implement their solutions quickly was
exceptional. The division engineers hailed his appointment, but others
with different backgrounds and skills were inclined to take a wait-and-
see attitude. They wondered how he would do in the demanding job of
running a division whose administrative and technical responsibilities
stretched beyond engineering problems. They knew that his familiarity with these non-engineering problems was essentially nil.

Approach: Dan was probably smart enough to realize that he had left a
position of engineer and advanced to a position of manager. Knowing
the details of one's job is an integral ingredient for making it on any job.
If you're in a job as an accountant, you have to know as much about
accounting as you can in relation to the requirements and specialities of
that job. The same goes for the job of engineer, lawyer, personnel
specialist, claims examiner, or computer specialist. A job as manager
needs special knowledge, also.

The problem with learning the details of a managerial job is that
there is so much to learn. A manager may be an accountant, engineer, or lawyer by profession, but when he becomes a manager, his
professional background is only one aspect of his job. It might be a
relatively unimportant aspect even though he was promoted into a
managerial position largely on the basis of the good job he did in
performing in his special field.

A manager has many responsibilities beyond those of his previous
occupational speciality. Being overattentive to that past occupation
can result in charges by his staff and others that he operates too
narrowly, that 'he still thinks he's an engineer.' True or not, this type of
accusation should be avoided because its negative implications conflict with the manager's need for broad-based staff support. Therefore,
in assuming a job as a manager, regard yourself as just that: a manager.
That is now your occupational speciality. Don't earn a reputation as a
lousy manager while you retain your reputation as a top-flight engineer.

Getting a mental fix that you are now a managerial specialist will
ease your entry into the world of managerial planning, personnel,

budgets, purchasing, recruiting, negotiating, production goals, training, and the other administrative details that make up a manager's life. Some managers do not like administrative details and consequently avoid learning about the intricacies of such important responsibilities as budget preparation, for one example. So what happens? If the manager fails to take time to understand such a major area of managerial importance, he will be unable to direct the progress in that area. He may in the short term be fortunate in having someone on his staff to provide direction for the responsibility he neglects. This may save him for a time, but if he doesn't know the important components of his job, his weaknesses identify themselves quickly. He becomes managerially vulnerable where he is weak. His overall management will be affected. It has to be affected. A lack of interest in the budget process can result in a lack of staff or funds to run the organization because he couldn't compete for available funds with other managers who do understand the importance of the budget process. Remember, too, that if a manager becomes known as one who lacks knowledge or interest on certain points, his staff soon shows less interest in those same areas.

To understand, to know, and to guide important aspects of your managerial responsibilities does not translate into your having to know the intricacies of those responsibilities in the same depth as the person under you who actually prepares the budget, for instance. But it does mean that you have to understand the process sufficiently so that you can supply the managerial direction to meet the goals for which you are striving. There is no way to gain this knowledge except to take the time and effort to acquire it and then to stay knowledgeable as changes take place. This knowledge will give you background to say yes or no on an informed basis. In the process, you'll be spreading the word about your method of operation. That will help ward off troublesome situations when people become angry with you because you don't know your job. Instead, you'll be a manager who shows evidence of having done your managerial homework.

Whatever you do, don't announce your pet managerial dislikes. Refrain from making public statements about them, such as 'I don't like to conduct staff meetings', or 'the budget process bores me', or 'I hate these administrative details'. You'll be vulnerable enough in privately disliking any major aspect of your job without proclaiming your weakness for all to know.

Letting People Go

*'If you are brave too often, people will
come to expect it of you.'*
Mignon McLaughlin

Problem: Bert searched diligently to fill one of his top supervisory
vacancies. The market was tight, but even though promising candidates were few, Bert felt that his extensive search had paid off when he
finally made his selection. Before long, however, he knew that his
choice was a mistake. The new employee did few things in the manner
that Bert had anticipated. Bert could have forgiven the new employee if
the resulting product had been adequate, but it hadn't. Something had
to give. Bert had never faced a problem like this before.

Approach: After you discover, like Bert, that one of your top managers
doesn't have it, you hate to admit that you made such a bad choice. But
if you don't face up to your mistake by trying to do something about it,
any initiative for solving the problem rests largely with the employee.
If you get lucky enough, he may move on to another job, but he just may
stay with you. In the meantime, he prevents you reaching office goals.
You know it and so does the rest of the office.

To do something positive, call in the employee to discuss his performance. Since he may be operating at the top limit of his capabilities,
don't assume that he knows he is doing a poor job. If he does know, he
also knows that he may lose his job, so don't expect a lot of voluntary
admissions from him. Instead, go over the job's requirements, your
expectations of their fulfilment, and an itemisation of the employee's
performance of them. Be low key and objective as you attempt to lay
the basis for a reasoned solution. Avoid any threat or possible sanction
in your initial statement. Seek the employee's side of the story. Try to
ferret out some area of agreement pointed towards improved performance. At the end of the meeting, reiterate what you expect, with
modifications in the light of his explanations. Set another meeting
date. Continue a schedule of meetings between the two of you as long
as there appears to be any hope that he can succeed in the job. Keep the
pressure on both of you to resolve the problem. This will help maintain
your determination to see the matter through.

If there is no substantial improvement after a reasonable time and
the employee's performance remains unsatisfactory, make the sacking
of the employee from his job as graceful and face-saving as you can for
him. After all, you picked him. If he can be relocated to use his abilities
better elsewhere in the organization, give him that opportunity. If he

cannot be relocated, give him the chance to resign. If he refuses to resign, inform him that his services will be terminated on a certain date. Work with your personnel office from the beginning so that you follow to the letter all necessary steps for his dismissal. Otherwise, you may prejudice the rights of the employee unintentionally and end up with charges against you for violating those rights.

Be sure to keep notes of your meetings with the employee. To sack an employee can be very sticky business, so you should have exact knowledge of what was said, and when, and by whom, should your actions be contested. Whatever you do, don't rely on your memory to save you in such a contest.

In taking the steps leading up to letting someone go, you will be monitored closely by your staff. And for good reason. It will occur to them that the same action may be initiated against one of them some day. So you will be the target of the brightest of spotlights. Never forget that you are dealing with the most basic bread-and-butter issue when you raise the possibility of dismissal from a job. Examine each step you take for fairness and compassion and, above all, be assiduously patient throughout this process, which by its nature is a highly charged emotional situation.

To let an employee go is a trying experience for all. Some managers cannot bring themselves to the point of going all the way. If you can, after doing your best to otherwise resolve the matter, you will acquire a managerial professionalism that can be acquired in no other way. You'll also raise your own opinion of your managerial ability by meeting head on a problem that many persons are prone to duck, to the detriment of themselves, the affected employee, and the organization.

Listening to Others

*'Personally I'm always ready to learn, although I do
not always like being taught.'*
Winston Churchill

Problem: Lucy brimmed with ideas, so when she took over as division chief, she relished the opportunity of communicating her ideas to her staff. She had definite views on how she wanted to run the division, and she let the staff know those views. At staff conferences she did most of the talking, and her staff quickly learned the futility of trying to contribute any ideas of their own. She regarded such expressions as opposition to her.

Approach: Lucy has forgotten that a manager has no corner on good ideas. If she or any manager could overhear a staff bull session when the boss is the subject of discussion, she would find her leadership ability questioned, at the very least, and, at worst, totally dismissed. Hard as it may be to accept, nobody is perfect, not even a manager who performs exceptionally well. Yet it is easy for a manager to become enchanted with her own ideas to the exclusion of those of others. Successful management calls for team work. A manager who does not listen to her staff finds they no longer bother to share their ideas with her. Such a one-person show may work for a while, but eventually every manager needs the benefit of the opinions and feedbacks of others. Staff silence does not constitute endorsement of the boss's every view.

When you listen to the opinions of others, you must do more than grant them an opportunity to be heard. You must show that you respect those opinions even if you disagree. If you ask for the opinion of one of your staff and then state 'that's completely wrong', you communicate lack of respect and a put-down for the speaker's opinion. Even a half-baked idea put forth sincerely has to be treated with tact to keep the lines of communication open. Ridiculing a half-baked idea is a good method for barring better-baked ideas. Receptivity to thoughts and ideas of others is best shown by careful listening, proper questioning, and managerial follow-up as the occasion warrants. To sustain lively dialogue between manager and staff shows respect and support.

When you establish this ambiance of respect and support, you run into the problem of how to handle the employee who always wants to talk, sometimes on the subject, but more often not. Instead of telling him to be quiet, don't put him down, but explain that inconsequential remarks will be better considered at another time. And then move on. If his remarks are to the point but he dominates the discussion too long, a simple 'that's a good point, now let's hear from others' provides your opening to call on others. While you are being a good listener, you still steer the discussion.

If you work yourself into a position where the staff rarely provides an opinion or feedback, do the obvious and start asking individual staff members for their opinions on specific subjects in staff meetings and elsewhere. Show that you want to hear from them by being attentive to their replies. If you have largely dominated the staff with your own opinions in the past, don't expect them to boil over with enthusiasm at your reversal of behaviour. It will take some time to win their trust and confidence. You will have to consciously hold yourself back whenever the old urge to dominate the discussion emerges while you develop your listening skills.

Lunch Time Renewal

'Somebody's boring me . . . I think it's me.'
Dylan Thomas

Problem: Joel felt deprived because he never had any private time in his job as manager. He was constantly involved with other people in carrying out his responsibilities. He even spent his lunch hour with members of his staff or with other persons some way connected with work. This non-stop work day left him mentally and physically exhausted by the time he got home at night. Even though he liked his work, he wished he had a break during the day.

Approach: Joel could make his lunch time a daily period of personal renewal. Lunch time is free time, a time to do and be what he, you, anyone wants to be. Out of force of habit you can spend your lunch hour with those you see in the office daily. That makes your lunch hour a continuation of the work day even if you don't talk business all the time. You can also eat with others from outside your immediate office who may or may not be interested in discussing business. Or you can grab a quick bite on your own and plan your own lunch time events.

Consider the possibilities during a lunch time on your own. Since your job as manager keeps you close to your desk without much physical activity, a brisk lunch time walk is a good stimulant to launch the afternoon. A visit to a book store, a department store, or an art gallery can break the work chain. Midday concerts and street-side entertainment are popular in large cities. You can just relax by sitting on a bench in the open and soak up sun and watch the passing parade. Plan a 'secret' lunch with your spouse at a fashionable restaurant. Make up a list of other lunch time diversions that are available in your area. However you spend your lunch hour, use the time to recharge your batteries for the rest of the day.

If you find that you're not looking forward to a continuation of your present lunch time pattern, change it to something more inviting. It's easier to go along with what you've been doing because it takes some gumption to announce to your regular luncheon companions that you're going to try something different. Like everything else, after the first jolt, nobody will pay attention to the change. Try it.

Making Things Happen

'Not to decide is to decide.'
Harvey Cox

Problem: Bridget called a meeting of her key staff the day after she became the section manager. There were policies that she wanted to announce and several items that she wanted the staff to follow up on. Because the last section manager had antagonised the staff by setting rigid deadlines for tasks, Bridget decided not to impose a specific deadline for the tasks she gave the staff at the first meeting. Instead, she asked the staff to get the completed items to her 'as soon as possible'. Her idea of 'as soon as possible' was one or two days, although she kept that to herself. The staff's idea of 'as soon as possible' was when they got around to it in a few weeks, or maybe never.

Approach: Bridget's concern about the previous manager's imposition of deadlines was misplaced. She learned that, human nature being what it is, a manager's delegation of tasks does not guarantee the completion of that task. To assure completion, both manager and employee have to understand what is supposed to happen, who's going to be responsible for making it happen, and the time by which it is to happen.

In order to make things happen by a specific time, a manager has to include a definite deadline for completion when she delegates. Without such a deadline the result will be an open-ended completion date, and the work may be relegated to the 'not urgent' pile. To be fair both to yourself and to your staff, specify whether you want a brief or detailed work product back on your desk – and when you want it. If what you want is not obvious, be sure to state the objective of the task; for instance, 'I want something that I can send to all new customers.'

The same clarity on what action is expected needs to be stated at the close of any meeting or discussion where further action is required. Be sure that you summarize the results of the meeting, make followup dates and set due dates. Without an action summary at the end of the meeting, you can be quite sure that things won't happen the way you want them to happen. Why should they, when no one has been given the responsibility to do something by a certain date? For those meetings where no followup action is necessary, end the meeting by so stating.

Very little ever happens in the work-a-day world or any other world without a plan to make it happen. Each delegation, each meeting, and each discussion creates a break point for action to begin. But action probably won't start unless there is a plan for making it occur. Make the who-what-when action summary one of your routine management tools.

Making Your Own Telephone Calls

'Inject a few raisins of conversation into the tasteless dough of existence.'

O. Henry

Problem: It was rare when Gus's secretary could connect him on the first try with the person Gus had asked her to telephone. Gus knew it wasn't her fault. People he called were busy managers like himself, and they weren't available to talk at the times he called. These frequent nonconnections tossed another degree of started-but-unfinished business into his day. If he could complete most of his telephone calls at his first attempt, his day would be more satisfactory.

Approach: Secretaries guard their prerogatives like anyone else. One favourite is to place their boss's phone calls. A new manager falls into this routine naturally. After all, like Gus, he now has a secretary as one of the services to make his life more productive. Why should he waste his time placing his own calls? But if the new manager takes time to consider the benefits of placing his own calls, he will make some if not all of his calls himself.

A manager has to protect the use of his time. He also has to arrange the best sequence in which to use that time. If his secretary places his calls, that sequence becomes unpredictable. For example, look at the typical patterns for time usage when Gus's secretary cannot make the connection with the person she calls: (1) the person is not at his desk, so the call will be returned at some later time; (2) the person cannot answer because he is in conference or on another call. Your call will be returned later; (3) the person is at his desk and available, but *his* secretary wants to delegate your call to someone else. Because most uncompleted phone calls fall into one of these categories, they add yet another complication to a manager's existence. The return call from the person you phoned in the first instance may likewise find you unavailable or no longer interested in talking to him. You may have solved the problem through other channels.

When a manager places his own calls, several things act to minimize the foregoing problems. The fact that the manager is calling takes the call out of the routine secretary-to-secretary category and gives it a different status to the secretary on the receiving end. She is talking to a real live boss. This allows you to negotiate with her. If her boss is on another call, ask her how long she thinks he will be. If she estimates a short time, ask to hold until he's finished. Meanwhile, you sign correspondence or sort items on your desk. If he's in conference and your subject is urgent, ask her to slip him a note while you wait because this is something he needs to know. If the person is out of the office, pin down his return time and tell the secretary when you plan to call back. This keeps you in control of your own time, and the secretary will expect your call and alert her boss to expect it. If the secretary wants to switch your call to someone else, but you do not want to speak to anyone other than her boss, you may be able to persuade her to put you through to him.

To place your own calls is not only efficient use of your time, but it also gives you a chance to get acquainted with those secretaries who can smooth communication routes to their bosses. Being known and liked by the secretaries makes your calls more like a friend calling a friend than just one more business call.

Mixing with the Staff

*'The perpetual obstacle to human
advancement is custom.'*
John Stuart Mill

Problem: When Bud was in the nonmanagerial ranks, one of the events he liked least was being called to the boss's office. He usually tightened up as he approached that office. When he got there, he usually had to hang around while the boss finished a phone conversation or completed other business. As he sat there waiting, Bud realized that the boss could really have little regard for Bud's time. But now that Bud was in a managerial position, he found he treated his staff much the same way his old boss had treated him. Maybe, he thought, his staff didn't mind such apparent disregard quite as much as he had.

Approach: The usual personal contact between a boss, such as Bud, and an employee is when the boss summons the employee to his office or when the employee seeks an appointment with the boss in the boss's office. Traditionally, a boss isn't found going to an employee's work area to discuss a problem.

But what's wrong with the boss actively seeking out one of his employees by going to that employee to talk to him? Well, in an office of any size, it just doesn't occur to the boss to do business that way. The customary way is less time consuming for the boss; it's evidence of status and the pecking order; and then there's the 'that's the way it's always done' syndrome.

A boss who, on occasion, seeks out his employees by going directly to them to discuss an office project shows a refreshing willingness to engage in an open relationship with his staff. The formality of reporting to the boss's office is replaced by the informality of the boss plopping down in an employee's work area to discuss a problem within hearing of other employees. This exposure permits other staff members to see and hear the boss in action, a scene usually confined to the sanctity of the boss's office. The boss is then seen as one who is willing to break away from the more traditional boss-employee role, and he does it without giving up anything but tradition. Such action opens the door to the possibility of better rapport that is not encouraged in the more traditional relationship.

In going to an employee, the boss places himself in the midst of the work force. He can observe things he would not ordinarily see and can measure the pace of the office from a different perspective.

Granted, such action takes more time and effort. There's even an element of uncertainty involved in moving out of your own territory. And you can't and probably won't want to do it often. But the novelty it adds to the office routine is worth the effort.

Motivating

*'The hopeful man sees success where others see
failure, sunshine where others see shadows and
storm.'*

P. S. Marden

Problem: Art was the best when it came to managerial procedures. He developed steps to implement new programmes and to redesign existing ones; he established checkpoints of staff accountability; he created innovative forms to track work progress. He had a procedure for everything, and useless red tape did not bog down his staff. Still, with all of his procedural talent, he had trouble getting his staff to meet the goals of his organization. He worked harder than any manager in the organization, but his staff didn't respond to his leadership.

Approach: Art's managerial procedures did not include leadership with motivation. Staff motivation is one of the outstanding contributions a manager can make to his organization. It may be his greatest contribution.

Motivation is the ability to stimulate yourself and others to action. If you aren't stimulated yourself, you'll never motivate others. They may be motivated, but not because of you. If you're not churned up and enthusiastic about what you are doing and what you want to accomplish, your staff will sense that lack. If you aren't motivated, why expect your staff to be?

Motivation is believing – believing that you can develop the best possible staff – that you can meet ambitious work goals, that the organization can reach the highest level of performance, that you can overcome obstacles, that you can succeed. In short, believing in what you're doing.

But motivation is even more than believing. It's practising your beliefs. If you believe you can have a top flight staff, you establish recruitment, training, and promotion polices to develop such a staff. You implement similar policies in other areas under your control to achieve your goals. You do more than declare high goals: you begin the work required to attain them. In the process you exude the determination that marks you as a motivated leader. Others catch your motivation because you inspire them and because you hold them accountable for meeting the standards you have set.

Motivation is more than a statement of 'wow-what-we're-doing-is-so-important!' A commitment to excel is one element of motivation.

Knowledge of the job is another. So is your support of your boss's goals. There are others, but these are the most obvious.

You find that those both above and below you recognize not only when you are motivated yourself, but also when you motivate others. You radiate self-confidence and your organization earns the reputation of 'winner'. There is no one way to motivate, since motivation takes many forms. Some persons motivate through fear and intimidation. Others through respect and trust. Some through exhortation. Different people respond to the same stimuli in different ways. What works for some may or may not work for you, but if you, yourself, enthusiastically respond to a certain type of direction, you've probably discovered the method that will be effective for you to use in inspiring others. Think of those persons who have motivated you most and why.

I learned the most about effective motivation from the best boss I ever had. He was a superb motivator. When he interviewed me for the job, he told me he wanted me in the job. When I reported for duty, he reiterated how glad he was to have me on his staff and how much confidence he had in my ability. He gave me general guidelines for what he wanted done, lots of rope with which to accomplish those goals, and plenty of encouragement. He did not spell out details about what my role was to be; he gave me goals to achieve. He held me fully accountable to achieve those goals, but he let me know he expected me to do so as a matter of course. His trust in me made me want to extend myself to please him. Then he rewarded me for doing the very things I had so enjoyed accomplishing. He saw to it that I received both monetary and honorary awards. He praised my abilities to other managers in the organization. He supported me fully and I knew it, so I strove ever harder to fulfil his aims. Now that's motivation!

Negotiating

'Let us begin anew, remembering on both sides that civility is not a sign of weakness, that sincerity is always subject to proof. Let us never negotiate out of fear. But let us never fear to negotiate.'

John F. Kennedy

Problem: A part of Sal's division was in the process of being unionized at the time he became chief. When the union came into being, Sal and an employee from the personnel department represented management in negotiations of a long list of demands by the union. Sal thought the demands were outrageous and so did his top managers. When the negotiations opened, he decided to take a very hard line against the union's demands. He would yield on very little so he could prove to them that they couldn't push him around just because he was the new boss.

Approach: Sal can't learn to negotiate successfully until he understands the basic principles of that skill. The very poorest possible strategy is to close one's mind from the outset to the demands of the other side. This only imbues the process with hostility from the beginning. To agree to negotiate implies a willingness to agree to some demands of the other side if they will reciprocate. Thus, terms of a mutually agreeable settlement can be discussed. Without the willingness to agree, negotiations are a sham. Negotiation, to be successful, means that every party gains something in the final settlement.

The successful negotiator follows the same formula for any negotiating session. The first step is *preparation*. He knows precisely each point his side wants to win in that session, and he estimates precisely what the other side hopes to win. Then he strikes a compromise in his mind for each issue on which the sides differ. He knows exactly how much each side can afford to give up in order to gain on another issue. Just knowing these 'stop points' gives the negotiator self-confidence that shows to the others and that in itself can scatter the opposition if those persons are not equally prepared. You would be surprised at how many times negotiators arrive at the negotiating table without having thought through these rudimentary points. But, even so, don't assume, at least at the start, that your opposition is less prepared than you are. Other preparatory tactics are: Try to hold the negotiations on your own turf and plan the seating arrangements in advance, so that you sit in the 'take charge' position and have a key associate on either side of you.

Have as few participants as possible to reduce distractions and to help keep the talks on track.

After preparation comes action. Your attitude at the negotiating table should be about the same as it is when you play poker. Don't give your hand away. For instance, be specific when you make an offer. I once participated in a negotiating session where an unskilled negotiator on the other side announced he would agree to a settlement anywhere between $100 thousand and $200 thousand. Naturally, I jumped at the end figure most favourable to our side, as would anyone.

No matter how well prepared you are and how carefully you have laid your plans, the actual session can produce surprises. Be sufficiently flexible to take advantage of unexpected turns of events and change your plans where necessary. Learn all you can at each session about the participants' objectives and their personalities in anticipation of your preparation for the next session. Summarize the results of each meeting at the end of it and then have your secretary type up the results and distribute them to all participants as soon as possible after the meeting. Always meet with participants on your side immediately before and after each negotiating session to clear up any possible misunderstandings on negotiating strategy. Take the initiative to adjourn for a meeting during the session itself as often as needed.

The opportunities for a manager to participate in negotiations, apart from formal conferences, are many. Not a day goes by without a manager finding himself negotiating something within the range of normal managerial responsibilities. How well a manager fares in his everyday negotiating role depends on the development of the same basic skills used in more formal negotiations. It is unusual for a good manager not to be a good negotiator since knowledge of human behaviour is needed in both pursuits.

New Employees

'Treat people as if they were what they ought to be and you help them to become what they are capable of being.'

Johann W. von Goethe

Problem: Ken started to notice new faces in his division shortly after he became chief. Except for the occasional recruit in a top position, he had no idea of the new employees' names, their skills, or their functions. They seemed to know who he was, but he did not know them. He finally took to introducing himself to any new employee he saw in the corridor or on the elevator. These exchanges were always on the wing and not much to Ken's liking. He wished he could meet the new employees as they joined.

Approach: Any person who has had more than one job knows there is no single way to baptise a new employee on his first day on the job. One job makes for one way. Two jobs make for two ways. Three jobs make for three ways. It is to the benefit of the organization, though, to try to make the first day as pleasant as possible.

From a manager's viewpoint, as Ken found out, since the organization cares about its new employee, the employee should be apprised of this concern. Welcoming the new employee so that he radiates a good feeling about his new job requires managerial planning. Once you have made the commitment to hire someone, a personal letter addressed to him at his home before his first day on the job is a thoughtful touch. Such a letter could reduce the number of people who don't turn up on what was supposed to be the first day of reporting on the job. Enclose a packet of information about your organization – an annual report, descriptive brochures, a company magazine. This gives the new employee a better understanding of the goals and accomplishments of the organization he is joining. In your letter, mention the important role he is to play in furthering those goals and how you are looking forward to his joining the organization.

The first day is a suspenseful experience for even an experienced job holder. Make that day as comfortable as possible by extending your own welcome first thing. Institute a policy of introducing each new employee to his fellow employees. Make sure at least one fellow worker accompanies him to lunch and coffee breaks on that first day. Don't assume that this will occur without a specific procedure to make it happen. When introductions are completed, hand the employee a fact sheet outlining such basic information as starting and leaving times, lunch hours, coffee breaks, what to do when reporting in sick, and whom to contact for answers to questions that are not covered by the fact sheet. If the job requires training or orientation, spell out the details in the fact sheet.

Giving the employee full information before he is assigned any work will ease the impact of the first day while laying the stage for a working relationship based on fact instead of rumour.

Offensive Employees

'A problem well stated is a problem half solved.'
Charles F. Kettering

Problem: As he was introduced to each employee in the unit, Bruno, the new chief, observed that Igor, one of the unit's highest ranking employees, had a strong body odour. Bruno soon learned that Igor's job required much public contact, and thus he was probably offending persons outside the office as well as his fellow workers. Igor's immediate supervisor admitted that neither he nor, as far as he knew, any other supervisor had ever told Igor to do something to correct his body odour.

Approach: At one time or another every office has an employee who has an offensive body odour or who has some other unpleasant personal problem. On that Bruno can rely. As usual, there are several ways to tackle the problem. You can ignore it, although the power of the smell in this case would make that hard to do. You can rationalize that to object to body odour is a modern phenomenon developed since the inventions of indoor plumbing, running water, deodorants, and all that stuff. Offensive body odour was also considered a badge of honour by the hippies of the sixties. However, the problem will remain as long as you only rationalize it.

As a manager, though, you may feel responsible for solving what really is not a funny problem. Here's a personal problem, a problem of offensive odour (it could be any other offensive personal problem) that is present constantly and intrudes into the privacy of others, and yet neither bosses nor fellow employees want to 'offend' the perpetrator by telling him to do something to correct the problem.

In my first managerial brush with this problem, my boss brought it up as just another managerial problem that needed my attention. First, he called me in as the supervisor of the person. He asked if I was offended by my odoriferous charge. I said I was. He asked if others on my staff were bothered. I said they were. Had I spoken to the employee? No, I hadn't. Why hadn't I? Well, it was such a delicate subject that I was embarrassed to bring myself to speak to the employee about it – I didn't want to hurt the employee's feelings. Did I think the problem would go away by itself? No, I didn't. At that point, my boss told me to go to the employee and order him to solve the problem. He did remind me to be gentle in my admonitions until I found out if the body odours arose from health problems beyond the person's control. I gritted my teeth and followed through on my boss's request. Telling that employee was one of the most difficult things I ever had to do.

The situation with my subordinate did show improvement, but it required my supervisory persistence until the offensive odours disappeared completely. No health problem was involved, and the odours disappeared by degrees. First, the employee started to use a deodorant daily. Then he began to bath regularly. Then he replaced his long-soiled clothing by degrees. Eventually, the noticeable odour was gone.

Several days after I had first discussed the problem with him, I happened to walk in the direction of his desk. He saw me approach and whipped out a can of spray deodorant from his desk drawer. He raised his arm and sprayed first one armpit and then the other right through his clothing. Talk about being responsive!

In later years when I would run into employees with this and other personal problems offensive to those around them, I never saw such a problem resolve itself. It never went away unless a supervisor insisted that the employee take action to solve the problem. Once corrected, the problem always seemed simple, and the supervisor basked in the perfume of success. But that's true of many management problems.

Office Space

'If it were not for space, all matter would be jammed in one lump and that lump wouldn't take up any room.'

Irene Peter

Problem: Before his promotion to division manager, Leroy had longed for a private office. He believed he needed that privacy to perform his best. As division manager he finally had his own office, but he had to face a staff that assumed he would be sympathetic to their requests for private offices. He was. But after he reviewed the division's budget, he realized that construction of additional private offices was not financially feasible. When Leroy told his staff of this, they reasoned that Leroy was like all the former bosses and would give them the same old runaround on solutions to their space problems.

Approach: The managerial responsibility of solving space problems is never mentioned during a job interview or on a job description. And these are problems. If you're the manager and you ignore these problems, your staff will accuse you of being insensitive, uncaring, and inhibiting the production goals you're always pushing the staff to meet. If you do get concerned about solving the problems of office space, you will find that the search for solutions is time consuming and that good solutions are hard to come by.

After all your concern, you find that no solution to the space problem is permanent. But if you give up in disgust, you still cannot duck those problems because they are right there in full view each day. Even if you turn a blind eye to the problems, your staff will be there to remind you repeatedly that the problem still exists.

These problems fall into several categories, none of which stretches the imagination: The space is too crowded. There's no privacy. It's too noisy. It's too hot. It's too cold. It's poorly located. It's too dimly lighted. It's too brightly lighted. It's not as good as the other offices in the organization.

Whether you, as a manager, consider a space problem real or imagined is unimportant. The problem has to be viewed through the eyes of the individual who is complaining. To him, the complaint is very real. Suppose, for example, that you investigate a complaint that a part of the office is too cold. You personally prefer your work space to be cool. Hence, you might be inclined to decide that the complaint is not justified. Unfortunately, you will never be able to convince the complainant that his work space is warm enough because you think so. The first rule, then, is to sympathize with the complainant. While this policy may endorse the complainant's belief that he has a problem, you have shown that you are concerned. This, in itself, may be a novel reception by management.

Once you've voiced your concern, take steps to do something about the complaint. For followup purposes, appoint someone on your immediate staff, someone with an abundance of patience and good sense, to be the primary contact point for space complaints and space planning. That person's job will be to work with the building management people, to answer complaints, to consult with office space experts, to prepare space cost estimates and budget needs, and to anticipate long-range office space requirements. This procedure, coupled with staff discussions for possible solutions, will direct this most vexatious of problems into a positive channel. In the process, you'll learn a good deal about the handling of a difficult problem.

On Being Yourself

*'It is the chiefest point of happiness that
a man is willing to be what he is.'*
Desiderius Erasmus

Problem: Marge's enthusiasm for her new job as section chief began to
wane on the day her predecessor came back to visit and advised her to
avoid being soft in managing her staff. 'Take a tough stand,' he said, 'or
they'll walk all over you.' This was soon after her deputy advised her to
go easy on her unit chiefs even though their production had fallen far
short of the section's goals, according to the monthly report just
completed.

Approach: As Marge learned, when a new manager takes over, advice
on how to manage is apt to come in generous portions. It comes in any
number of gradations between the two extremes: 'be tough' or 'be soft'.
And as a manager's career ages, she finds that advice keeps rolling in for
her to pick and choose.

Listening to staff advice is one thing. Following it is another. Those
giving advice have their own reasons. Their motivation may be to help
you, and the direction in which they point may be the right direction.
And maybe not. Remember, whatever action you take, right or wrong,
you are responsible for the result, regardless of who advised you. So
proceed cautiously before you decide on the brand of leadership you
adopt in the beginning of your management career and as your career
progresses.

Certainly, in an organization of any appreciable size, you have to rely
on the advice of others. But for leadership tone you alone have to decide
whether you want to be tough or soft or somewhere in between. You
alone have to account for results of your operating style. That style
cannot be set by others because then it is not your style. And because
you are responsible for the organization's ultimate success or failure,
the style should be yours. On occasion, your style may coincide with
that of someone who gave you advice. That's fine, so long as you regard
the style as yours, feel right with it, and it works.

The importance of operating in your own style is that you have to be
at ease with yourself to be effective. You really can't be anyone else as a
boss any more than you can be anyone other than yourself in any other
area of life.

Your style does not have to be inflexible. On the contrary. Life is
change. Still, if someone wants you to see a situation as white, and you
don't see it that way, don't change your vision. Later, perhaps you will

agree with him, but now you don't. You have to know your own limits. If someone advises you to be tough, but it isn't within you to act that way at that time, don't. Be yourself. Effective management requires integrity, conviction, knowledge, courage, awareness, timing. These qualities determine how you react in any situation. Put the advice of others through your personal filter before using it. If you feel right with the result, you may want to follow it. But don't accept any advice and act on it without first analysing it and adapting it to your own style.

On Getting Angry

'The cat in gloves catches no mice.'
Benjamin Franklin

Problem: Nick was one of those even-tempered managers who was never ruffled by anything. No one could remember ever seeing him angry. When something went wrong the staff didn't shy away from good old Nick. He knew how to take it. If a mistake was made, no matter how serious, the staff was confident that Nick would not take it out on them like a lot of bosses would. In explaining Nick's behaviour, some of his staff said that he didn't really care much about anything, while others defended him as just an extremely nice guy.

Approach: Nick's temperament is at one end of the scale for bosses. The opposite extreme is that of the boss who gets a reputation for having emotional outbursts regularly. No one likes to be the victim of a boss's wrath. An employee who has felt such wrath knows its shrivelling effect. New bosses, particularly, may forget that effect and find themselves indulging in temper tantrums as a substitute for analysing what's wrong and how to correct it when they meet new, trying situations.

If you become known as a manager who takes his anger out on his staff, the reaction of the staff will be predictable. They will try to avoid you. Mutual trust, respect, and communication will suffer. The ability to meet the goals of the office will be affected. The very aims that the boss's outbursts were designed to correct will be more frustrated. The operation of the office on a foundation of anger and intimidation is self-defeating.

This does not mean that there is never an occasion for the boss to display emotional concern. Leadership that does not evidence an outward concern lacks a quality needed to uplift a staff to that extra effort. This is constructive managerial emotion as contrasted with destructive outbursts of wild anger.

An emotional commitment may be evidenced by the boss who gets angry when the occasion calls for it. This is a show of deliberate anger that is controlled, not contrived. If a boss is so even-tempered that he never gets cross at anything, his demeanour may bore his staff and dull their will to achieve. Getting cross without vindictiveness can be beneficial if used sparingly enough not to be a predictable pattern of conduct. Some situations demand a show of dissatisfaction. To get the most out of such an episode, though, the boss should follow with a programme to correct the problem that caused the emotional upset. Blowing up won't do it by itself.

If all this sounds calculating, it is, to the extent that the boss who doesn't keep control of a situation, even a display of emotion, will find his ability to manage limited. A manager always has to be alert to managerial limitations. The more the limitations, the more splintered the management, and the less likely that the goals of the manager will be met.

Overcoming Bureaucracy

'We can lick gravity, but sometimes
the paperwork is overwhelming.'
Wernher von Braun

Problem: Russ had never worked for an outfit like this before. When he became head of the division, he found it so enmeshed in red tape that solving any problem was difficult because the problem tended to sink from its own weight. The division staff, for the most part, accepted the fact that it was hard to get anything done. If Russ questioned the delay in completing a piece of work, the person questioned took refuge in the bureaucracy that engulfed the division. Russ found that many of the delays were not imposed by others, but were the result of the division's own rules, policies, and procedures. In effect, the staff had insulated itself against improvements.

Approach: Although the term *bureaucracy* is closely identified with government, no organization, governmental or nongovernmental, is immune from the disease. Bureaucracy, as Russ learned, consists of unwieldy administration. Bureaucracy involves lots of rules, lots of policies, lots of clearances, lots of delays, and lots of excuses before final action occurs – if ever.

Being a part of a bureaucratic organization provides manager and staff with a convenient scapegoat when things aren't working well. They can blame the bureaucracy – the cold, abstract, non-human, faceless bureaucracy – for their inability to deliver.

At the same time, an organization buried in bureaucracy provides an opening for a manager to try to cut through the bureaucracy. Consider the possibilities to reduce red tape in such a routine matter as replying to a letter of inquiry or complaint. Why does the reply have to be in writing? Answer: Because it has always been in writing. The written reply takes composing time, typing time, clearance time, mailing time. Time, time, time. Delay, delay, delay. As a manager, you can try experiments, on a pilot scale at first so you can monitor performance for any needed adjustments. Try answering certain types of correspondence by telephone. If it's not possible to make the connection by phone, have the person who actually handles the inquiry sign the reply rather than delay the answer by sending it through channels to be signed by someone higher up in the organization. Make it a practice to include the telephone number of the person signing the letter, along with a closing statement to call that number if further information is needed. Encourage the recipient to talk to a real, live human being identified by name in the reply.

When you identify who can be contacted, and at what phone number, for additional information on all correspondence, you crack the bureaucratic wall of anonymity. You're telling the recipient of each letter that your organization does care about him and his problem. Whoever handles the inquiry has extra motivation to perform well because he puts his name and reputation on the line. More important, you will have chipped away at some of the oppressiveness of the bureaucracy by showing that your organization is responsive.

Search for opportunities to humanize the way the organization does things. Do your own searching, but also ask your staff and outsiders who deal with your organization for suggestions to pierce the bureaucratic veil. Notch up your score for doing things faster and better. Keep in mind that when the rules and policies of the game (the 'game' being the work of your office) reach a point where there is no purpose to the game any more – just rules and policies – there's something awfully wrong. The opportunities to win the game, though, are there.

Performance Appraisals

'The fellow who never makes a mistake takes
his orders from one who does.'
Herbert V. Prochnow

Problem: Vicky had supervised Mary Laura for almost six months now. Mary Laura was not progressing on the job as well as Vicky had expected. She was deficient in several important areas, and instead of getting better with experience she showed no improvement. Mary Laura gave no signs that she was aware of her shortcomings. Well, Vicky thought, she would get Mary Laura when the annual appraisals of employee performance came due at the end of the year. Mary Laura didn't know it, but Vicky recorded each of Mary Laura's deficiencies as they occurred so that her annual appraisal would be devastating.

Approach: Although Vicky believes that only Mary Laura is failing to perform her duties adequately, in truth, Vicky is failing equally in her own performance. Formal appraisals of employee performance are scheduled in many organizations annually to help determine employee promotions and training needs. They are used by management as a basis for dismissal only after earlier formal steps have been taken to alert the employee to her deficiencies and after all efforts on the parts of the employee and her supervisor have failed to improve the employee's performance. *Informal* appraisals of employee performance are everyday occurrences that influence the formal annual appraisal. Every time an employee types a letter, submits a report, or briefs her boss, the employee's performance is judged, consciously or unconsciously, by the boss.

Anticipation of an upcoming formal appraisal, which will go into the employee's official file, can build up tension between the employee and her supervisor to a point that the benefits of the appraisal are destroyed by the time the formal session is held. This is particularly true when the supervisor dreads the eyeball-to-eyeball, closed door, sit-down appraisal as much as the employee. No appraisal, however, should cause that high an emotional pitch. A supervisor who waits as long as a year to tell her employee that her performance is so poor that her job is in jeopardy has perverted the reasons for employee appraisal. The overriding reason is to help improve an employee's performance and thereby develop a better organization. To do this, the appraisal process has to be a continuing supervisory responsibility, not merely a once-a-year session fraught with tension on both sides. The good and the bad aspects have to be discussed constructively throughout the work year.

A running dialogue is thus established between supervisor and employee so that no surprises arise at the annual appraisal. The formal appraisal then serves as a cap on a relationship that has been nurtured all year long.

If you are a supervisor who is displeased or bothered by an employee's job performance, let him know about it, but don't nag. For example, if the employee's production is below that of others doing similar work, discuss this frankly, yet gently, with him. After trying to determine the reasons for his poor performance, let him tell you what he will do to improve and, in turn, tell him what you will do to help him. If improvement doesn't result within a reasonable time, discuss the consequences of continued substandard performance. One consequence may be to switch him to work more suitable to his abilities. The most extreme consequence is dismissal. Do not take for granted that the employee understands the range of consequences. Explain them to him. Then follow through on any sanctions. If you are 'all talk' and the employee senses this, the possibility of improvement is hindered from the start.

The performance appraisal procedure, whether on-going or formal, has to be a two-way communication to work. Instead of coming down heavily on an employee who needs help, try to create a climate in which he can improve. One opening is to ask the employee how he thinks he's doing on his job. His self-appraisal may equate with yours. Such an opening doesn't always work, but the stage is set for discussion. Keep your appraisal sessions conversational rather than as supervisory monologues. This will encourage discussion of problem solutions versus issuing of supervisory edicts. You could even learn that some changes in your own conduct could help improve the employee's performance. Stranger things have happened.

Personal Policy Letters

'To know all things is not permitted.'
Horace

Problem: Ruth felt challenged by her inability to consistently communicate significant policies and directions to her staff. Because of staff turnover and the difficulty of assembling the whole staff at one time, oral communication wasn't working. While she didn't want to create another impersonal office procedures type of manual, she did want to be able to permanently record her personal management policies.

Approach: Ruth could consider writing an occasional message to her staff in the form of a personal policy letter. Since she would be the only one to write them, her own style would be imprinted on each one.

In creating your policy letter, restrict the first one to an announcement of the purpose of the letters, which is to improve communication from you to the staff on various topics as you view them from your perspective as manager, but explain that you will welcome ideas for letter topics. Explain that there will be no fixed schedule for the issuing of the letters, but they will be released when you perceive the need. Each one will be brief and limited to one subject.

A personal policy letter opens up an opportunity for a manager to express her views on subjects that normally are not discussed in the more conventional office memos. For example, assume a new year is beginning and your organization finished well down the scale in accomplishments for the past year compared with similar organizational units. A year-end policy letter could state why you believe your organization performed as it did, how you plan to help improve that performance in the coming year, the benefits that will be gained by an improved performance, and the problems connected with a continued below-par performance. Additional policy letters on the same subject could be issued periodically to keep the staff up to date as the year progresses.

Since topics for policy letters are under your exclusive control, begin a list of the ones you deem worthy of a personal policy letter. Then list priorities. Add to it as new topics occur to you. Some letters might cover your policy on completed staff work, deadlines, training, promotions, or dealing with the public. Do not try to set forth detailed operating procedures in the letters, or they will start to resemble just another operating manual.

Six months after you've launched your policy letter series, evaluate its effectiveness. Has it strengthened communication? Can you detect improvements in staff performance that might have stemmed from the letters? Do you enjoy communicating through the letters? If not, what's lacking? Are you getting policy letter feedback? Have you been able to communicate significant ideas, opinions, and directional signals more effectively with the letters than before? Poll your staff on their opinions of the letters.

After I started my own policy letters, the greatest support I received for continuing them came from my top management staff. They would come to me individually with suggestions to reissue an updated version of a previous letter or issue a new one on a fresh topic. This type of sustained support persuaded me to make the personal policy letter a permanent part of my own management kit.

Personalizing Your Office Decor

*'We forfeit three-fourths of ourselves
in order to be like other people.'*
Arthur Schopenhauer

Problem: Except for being larger, Gretchen's office looked no different from the other offices in her division, even though she was the chief. She had the same basic furniture, the same colour scheme, the same standard wastepaper basket, and the same undistinguished-looking carpet. She wanted to change the appearance of her office, but grew discouraged when she considered how difficult it was to secure any supplies or office equipment through the central supply office. She resigned herself to living with the uninspiring surroundings and busied herself with the work of the division.

Approach: I don't want to sound chauvinistic by suggesting that Gretchen might want to build a nest in her office, because she has a good idea in trying for some individuality. A manager spends almost as much time in her office as she does in her home. While she gives great care to furnishing and landscaping her home, ordinarily she spends little care on personalizing her office.

You can personalize an office the same way you personalize your home. Your office can look like an extension of your home, or it can have a completely different decor. Such surroundings are yours for the planning and execution.

Many offices look like cluttered cells – dull and drab, with few expressions of individuality. One of the improvements you can make most easily (that quality alone should be persuasive) is to personalize your office so that you can work in an atmosphere that expresses you.

To begin the transformation, install a table lamp or floor lamp, or both. After all, who ever had a living room with just fluorescent lights or an overhead light bulb? A lamp or two, along with the fluorescents, if needed, sets a different tone for your office. Instead of hanging the usual ego-trip diplomas or awards, try mounting some inexpensive prints of the master artists. Or if you or a member of your family dabbles in art or a craft, display a sample or two of this original work. It's worthy of decorating your walls.

This is an opportunity to recycle objets d'art from your home or to purchase new ones for the office. Artistic impressions that exhibit your interest in birds, animals, or a hobby can provide a personal warmth for you during office hours and serve as a relaxing backdrop to the trials of the job.

Even if you have a carpeted office, the addition of a small rug helps to individualize your office further. And don't forget plants and other green stuff even if you don't have green fingers. Adopting an aspidistra tree for the office might give you the training you need to acquire fingers of that colour.

To provide a bit of whimsy, you might install a miniature basketball hoop and net on your wastepaper basket or a dart board on the back of your door. Your shooting percentage with waste paper balls or darts may hardly bolster your spirits, though.

Anyway, you have the idea. It's a fun project without end. As you express yourself this way, the staff will find excuses to visit your office for the pleasure they get out of peeking at your newest acquisition.

Plan for Tomorrow

'Our plans miscarry because they have no aim. When a man does not know what harbour he is making for, no wind is the right wind.'

Seneca (4 B.C.–A.D. 65)

Problem: As Esther marked her first anniversary as unit chief, she thought back to that day when she had taken charge. Her head spun with ideas to improve her new unit. Some of those early ideas were relatively simple and easily implemented. Others drifted to the back of her mind as she immersed herself in the routine work of the unit. With experience, she learned which areas in her unit needed strengthening, and she could even see where problems could be anticipated. However, she could not turn her attention to these trouble spots as much as she wanted because she was so busy with the everyday work of the unit.

Approach: Routine duties can take up so much of a manager's attention that she puts off implementing many of the new ideas that could help make those very duties easier. She doesn't really forget the potential improvements; she just postpones them, since the office is operating fairly efficiently without them. This is Esther's problem. If it is also yours, try to take a few moments from your routine tasks to focus on those areas you know need special attention.

Think for a moment of how many of your brilliant ideas you could put in motion tomorrow with only a phone call or a short memo. Jot down two or three and date the note. Then the first thing tomorrow morning, act on at least one of those items on your list even before you start your regular work. Try to act on each item during the day and cross it off when you complete it. Then, just before leaving time, again take a few minutes to jot down those nonroutine jobs you'd like to accomplish or start the next day. Transfer over any open items from the previous day. Force yourself to do this regularly at the end of your work day until it becomes a habit.

The items on your 'DO' list depend on you, but to use mine for example, they might appear as follows:

- Call MacBeth re get together
- Call Sullivan re training
- Talk to John re overspending
- Assess office space situation

They are only reminders like those on a grocery list, so they need not be lengthy. If you write your lists in a pocket notebook (mine is about 2 × 4 inches), you can carry it with you to use in case you're inspired to make a new entry at some other time or place. Note those fleeting ideas you have to improve your unit's operation.

The time required to implement your creative ideas may begin to impinge on the time you need for regular work. If so, place your priorities in their proper order and adjust your work load to accommodate the work on your 'DO' list. You will probably find that some of the routine work can be delegated or even eliminated.

After you establish the habit of using a daily work plan, you'll find you've gained control over parts of your job you thought were uncontrollable. You'll find, too, that you accomplish much more than you did before when you drifted along without the rudder of a written guide.

Pocket Diaries

'We must ask where we are and whither we are tending.'
Abraham Lincoln

Problem: The number of things that Connie had to keep track of since becoming a manager was maddening. She relied on her secretary to keep her regular appointments straight. She jotted down reminders of other events and kept them on her desk or in her handbag. Some coming events were not amenable to being noted in any of her or her secretary's reminder systems. With a travel schedule that often kept her out of the office, she was never sure that she had a record of all her future appointments.

Approach: Connie has now reached that point that comes in each person's rise through the hierarchy when it becomes important to record in the same place all one's nonroutine appointments; for instance, what you will be doing at 2:00 P.M. three weeks from this Thursday. It's important so that you remember scheduled events and don't schedule something else for the same time slot. The time for devising a system for writing down this information usually comes when a person assumes her first managerial position. Until then, unless she's unusually active, she can probably keep such matters straight in other ways.

Once you assume a managerial position, you enter a demanding time sphere. It's a sphere of meetings, conferences, budget cycles, appointments with people you want to see or who want to see you, briefings, travel, and speeches. You cannot handle such details well without an orderly system. One system is the pocket diary. These compact little booklets, available in stationers, provide calendars that project ahead for a year or more with room for notations to remind you of things you have to do each day at specific times. If you agree on March 14 to make a speech at the City Club at 2:00 P.M. on June 23, you enter that notation in the June 23 space block in your pocket diary. To remind you to prepare for the speech, you'll want backtrack notations such as a June 1 entry of 'start draft of 6/23 speech' and a June 15 entry of 'finish final speech draft and start dry run for 6/23'.

At the beginning of each month and each year, make a series of reminder entries in the diary for actions that you foresee. For instance, you can make notations on the proper dates for budget preparation, progress reports, performance ratings, and holiday schedules. And don't forget your relations' and friends' birthdays! In this way, your pocket diary can be a valuable planning guide.

One advantage of a pocket diary, compared to other reminder-type documents on which you may rely, is its portability. Compact in size and weight, you can carry it with you at all times in a pocket or handbag and use it wherever you are, whether in your office, at home, or a thousand miles away. Once you get the habit, you'll come to rely on the pocket diary so heavily that you'll feel lost without it.

Retain the used diary for each year as a summary in case you ever want to verify when some event took place.

Preparing for Meetings

'For purposes of action nothing is more useful than narrowness of thought combined with energy of will.'

Henry Frederic Amiel

Problem: Tom knew his job as section chief well, but he hated to present the required periodic oral and written briefings to his boss. These briefings, even with the help of his staff, never seemed to go over. Usually they were too long, overlapping, not incisive, and they were, Tom thought, poorly received. He worried about why his briefings were so inadequate since he tried to have his most knowledgeable staff members at the briefings and always told them to come fully prepared.

Approach: If you are subject to Tom's problem, the time to begin solving the next one is when the briefing meeting is announced. For instance, say the boss calls you on Tuesday. He wants a full briefing on an area within your responsibility at a meeting in his office one week from today. You may bring two staff members to the meeting with you.

Right after you receive the call, decide who you want to take with you to the meeting. Having these others accompany you does several things – at least it should, and, with proper direction, will. First, those who attend with you must prepare in advance. Second, their talents can be put on display to your boss. By placing the responsibility for preparation on those who work more closely to the project than you, you're more likely to have a successful briefing.

Between the time you receive the call and next Tuesday's briefing, your job is to develop the subjects to be included in the briefing and to see that their presentations have substance, balance, and order. Thus your boss can benefit from your knowledge and that of your staff. To accomplish this requires preparation or, to use governmentese, 'advance preparation'.

Ask the two staff members to come to your office for a meeting. Discuss with them your role and theirs in the briefing, lay out a tentative agenda, and set a schedule for finishing a fact sheet to distribute at the briefing. Fix a specific time for a dry-run session in your office to hear firsthand the briefing to be given to your boss. So that you are able to review the written materials beforehand, ask that they be given to you at least twenty-four hours before the prebriefing. Then take the time to review the material thoroughly before the dry-run briefing.

A dry-run briefing helps prevent laying an egg at the real meeting by permitting you to bolster any weak spots in the presentation. You use it to curb duplication and establish time limits for each participant. The rehearsal gives you insights into the quality of your staff and, by employing this procedure, you are engaged in staff development. The final result is a presentation at the real meeting that shows your boss that you and your staff do your homework.

Problem Employees

*'It is easy to be tolerant of the principles of other
people if you have none of your own.'*
                                    Sir Herbert Samuel

Problem: To acquaint himself with the division of which he was the
new chief, Evan asked each supervisor under him to brief him on the
duties and performances of every division employee. As he expected,
there were a variety of duties and a concomitant variety of performances of those duties. One employee, however, was so divergent from
the rest that he was set apart. His duties were vague and he was
virtually nonaccountable to anyone for his performance. He drew his
paycheque regularly and each year got an acceptable performance
rating. His supervisor said he had tried working with the employee but
that he was more than he or anyone else in the division could manage.

Approach: If, like Evan, you arrive upon the management scene to find
you have inherited a problem employee, you have several options. You
can forget about him and let him continue in his ways; you can try to
'reform' him; you can try to place him elsewhere in the organization;
you can hope that he leaves on his own; or you can try to get rid of him
completely.

A long-standing problem employee is an individual whom previous
supervisors have given up on. He reports to work in the morning and,
for the most part, does what he pleases as far as duties go. There is an
implicit understanding that he doesn't interfere with the supervisors
and they don't interfere with him. This peculiar status usually develops because a supervisor once tried to get rid of him, was unsuccess-
ful, and then decided not to fight the battle any more. The white flag of
management was raised and the employee recognized it. He may even
have been a capable worker at one time, but his special status squelches
the use of any abilities he possesses. Your first inclination will probably
be to 'do something' about this employee, in spite of the lack of
encouragement from others on your staff, especially if they will be
involved in any way.

For openers, if you want to 'do something', invite the employee,
along with his immediate supervisor, to meet with you for a get-
acquainted session. Tell him that you're starting your new job with a
clean slate. Mention your hopes and aspirations as the new boss. Ask
him his. See if you can strike a degree of rapport that might spark
emergence from his shell. If you're able to detect any interest, pick it up
from there. If you're not able to detect interest, make no threats, but

make it clear that you expect everyone to perform to prescribed standards of work. This is not an unreasonable statement to make no matter what the circumstances. Keep his supervisor fully accountable for any followup actions. There is no quick and easy solution to this type of problem. An employee who won't fit in, who's left to stew in his own juices, is an unhealthy employee from all sides, his included. But be fair. Give him a chance. A good chance. And resolve to stay with the problem until it is resolved in a manner better than just considering him the office oddball and letting him go at that. The problem he represents ranks among the hardest for a manager to solve. As you get into it deeper, you'll appreciate why others have let the problem ride.

Once you have seen a problem like this through, you'll feel better about yourself as a manager as you nurse your wounds. You'll know yourself better – and so will your staff.

Punctuality

*'There are two kinds of people in life – people whom
one keeps waiting – and people for whom one waits.'*
S. N. Behrman

Problem: Benson had a reputation for being chronically late to meetings. When the specified time of the meeting arrived, his boss, Manny, would ask, 'Where's Benson?' Then everyone would wait for Benson to arrive before the meeting could start. Manny would fume about the delayed start of the meeting. Benson would always apologize and offer an excuse for his tardiness. An otherwise good employee, Benson knew that Manny was upset with his tardiness, but he also knew that Manny never started a meeting until everyone was present.

Approach: Perhaps you've faced Manny's problem. You announce a one-hour staff meeting to start at 2:00 P.M. Six people, including yourself, are scheduled to attend. Ample notice is given to minimize attendance conflicts. For this meeting, no one reports any conflicts.

The time for the meeting arrives, but only three people are on time. Within a minute or two, another person arrives. Within five minutes, all but one person has arrived. The last person is eight minutes late. Just before he arrives, one of the persons who arrived on time steps out to make a phone call. The others wait restlessly for the meeting to begin. Finally the meeting can begin at 2:12 P.M. with all present.

This scene can happen repeatedly if a manager allows it to occur. If you let it happen over and over again, you give a good clue on how you regard the use of time within your organization and how you feel about when your staff meetings start.

Conversely, if you want to foster respect for punctuality and the meeting of deadlines, you couldn't start more directly than convening all meetings on time. If you follow this advice, give fair warning to your staff of your intent and then proceed to follow through, regardless of how many participants show up on time.

Once the policy is announced, start each meeting at precisely the designated time. Those who do not show up will soon be convinced of your punctuality. Even the most chronic late-comer may change his ways to avoid defying the boss with regularity. Those who are always prompt will continue to be prompt. They will appreciate your attempt to end tardiness.

With a policy of punctuality, the meeting takes on an air of importance from its inception. The time of the manager and each participant is recognized as important. If scheduled to last for one hour, the meeting is paced to conclude on time. This gives the boss an opportunity to orchestrate a tight meeting. The meeting has more meaning because trivial and extraneous matters are squeezed out of the discussion. If the meeting can end before the scheduled time, end it, and your reputation as a boss who values everyone's time will grow.

Quantifying Goals

*'Each morning puts a man on trial and
each evening passes judgment.'*
Roy L. Smith

Problem: Ted was impressed with the staff he inherited when he became chief of the unit. The staff was bright, enthusiastic, and genuinely helpful. He knew that the division's major shortcoming in the last few years was its inability to meet its production goals. Regardless of the staff's good qualities, he learned that they were not very concerned about their consistent failure to achieve production goals. Staff members believed that they produced a quality product and that quality offset the deficiency in meeting quantitative production goals. In the staff's collective opinion, production goals might be important to some, but to them they were no more than a numbers game that had little to do with qualitative success.

Approach: A manager, like Ted, who sees his staff deliver a quality product but who does not hold them accountable for quantifiable goals, will be unable to measure results objectively or effectively. Without such production goals, the manager's attempts to compare performance of one member of his staff with that of another become very much a subjective and chancy judgment. The lack of insistence on meeting quantifiable goals will ultimately affect the manager's ability to get a budget to support his shop because of the lack of quantitative results. Quantity and quality are not mutually exclusive.

A manager who communicates definite quantifiable goals to his staff and holds the staff accountable for reaching those goals provides an objective basis on which to measure performance. An old professor of mine once said that 'quantity begets quality'. That saying can apply here, but only when quantitative goals are fixed after consideration for quality and when the staff understands that both quantity and quality are work standards. Both manager and staff then know that these work standards are included as part of the performance appraisal process. Thus everyone is held to the mark for his part in attempting to achieve the organizational goals. To the achievers go the spoils.

Since production goals are usually set on an annual basis, they should be broken down into smaller time segments so that the manager and his staff can monitor the rate of performance as the year goes along. Therefore, have your staff prorate the annual goal into quarterly, monthly, and weekly goals. Chart the progress towards meeting them. This system keeps the goals visible at all times and can alert management to any bog-downs as well as to how well the work is progressing.

Of course, work progress will be the subject of frequent staff meetings. The manager has to resist turning these accountability sessions into problem-solving sessions. So take note of the problems raised, but keep your attention focussed on production goals. This approach will help to reduce excuses for failing to meet the goals. In addition, it will place the responsibility for problem solving where it belongs – at the level of management closest to the production line rather than in the lap of the top manager.

If the original production goals you've set appear to be absolutely unattainable after a reasonable effort to achieve them, revise those goals to a more realistic level. Admittedly, if you lower your goals this way, your boss and the other managers above you may cast a critical eye at you and your organization. But if you stick with impossible production goals until the original target date marking the end of the production period, their criticism is only delayed. It may be even more severe at the later date. If you don't bow to the inevitable and change your goals, the whole production goal process will have been demeaned. A tracking and accountability system is most forceful when production goals, though ambitious, appear to be attainable from the beginning and then are attained.

Quick Retrieval File System

*'The next best thing to knowing something
is knowing where to find it.'*
Samuel Johnson

Problem: Vance was generally pleased with the filing system in his section. He had directed the design of it after becoming section chief. There was one part of the system, though, that was still unreliable. This part showed itself most often when he received a telephone call about recent correspondence. If he asked his secretary to give him a copy to refresh his memory while the caller was still on the phone, sometimes she produced it, but just as often she couldn't. Frequently Vance couldn't answer the query from memory and had to call back later. Such a procedure wasted a lot of time, he reasoned.

Approach: Vance will have to solve this problem himself. When a manager needs the file copy of a piece of recent correspondence or report quickly, it's a good bet that he'll have trouble getting it if he relies on the office filing system, no matter how good that system may be. Even if the system is reliable, the manager can be delayed by the staff's inability to get a copy to him at a moment's notice. The reasons are understandable: his secretary may be away from her desk at the moment; the material may not yet be filed; or the exact date and subject matter of the material may not be known.

You will find that you usually need a file copy to refresh your memory so you can dispose of the matter then and there when you receive a phone call. A simple solution is to have an extra copy of the material near your phone. Establish a fifteen-day chronologically arranged personal file and keep it convenient to you and the phone. Retain copies of all outgoing correspondence you may be quizzed about in the near future, say in the next fifteen days. Because the file is kept by date, you can quickly thumb through to find a copy of your outgoing letter or report when necessary.

With a personal retrieval system, you will become known as a person who is responsive to callers and as a person who knows his job. Your secretary will be relieved of that frantic yell from you to 'get me a copy of that Jones letter', while you're trying to hold on to your caller. Another crisis may be avoided.

To keep this personal file manageable, go through it yourself each day to discard those materials over fifteen days old that you no longer expect to hear about. This pruning process will also refresh your memory about those items on which an inquiry is still possible.

Reorganizing

*'We trained hard ... but every time we were begin-
ning to form up into teams, we would be reorganized.
I was to learn later in life that we tend to meet any
new situation by reorganizing ... and a wonderful
method it can be for creating the illusion of progress
while producing inefficiency and demoralization.'*

Petronius (d. A.D. 66)

Problem: The division that Debra headed following Steve's transfer
fell far short of reaching its objectives for the second year in a row. Steve
had reorganized the division nine months before he left, but performance continued to slip. Some persons on Debra's staff advised her
to give the reorganization more time to work while others said that
the current system would never work and she should reorganize the
division. Meanwhile, Debra's boss pressed her to improve the performance of the division.

Approach: Poor Debra! She's caught between Scylla and Charybdis.
Usually when a new boss takes over, she can be relied upon to make
two statements: first, that she is impressed by the competence of the
staff and, second, that she has no plans to reorganize.

Shortly after making these statements, the boss initiates her first
move to reorganize and to bring in new people. It's an opportunity
many a boss finds irresistible. She can bring in new faces and hint that
more changes are in the offing and, most important, she knows that her
presence is recognized. She is on the scene, and everybody knows it.

Few bosses intentionally initiate the inefficiency and demoralization that Petronius identified two thousand years ago. Yet there is
hardly a more destructive tool than reorganization unless it is used
with caution. You can reorganize with a sledgehammer or a scalpel.
Usually a sledgehammer is used. That's why reorganization breeds
staff discontent. Anxiety impedes the work of the office and defeats
what should be the principal aim of a reorganization: to improve
performance. So unless improved performance results, the reorganization is a failure. Unfortunately, the scene is set for another
reorganization.

No matter how well-intended a reorganization may be, someone will
be hurt. The measure of a successful reorganization is to gain more than
is lost. Therefore, before a manager even hints at a reorganization, she
must assess the potential gains and losses. What's the real purpose of
the reorganization? Is it more than an ego trip? Who and what will

suffer? What will be the benefits? Do they outstrip the losses by a wide margin? If not, the reorganization may be doomed to failure and production will probably fall below the present rate, which ostensibly is already too low.

Obviously, from time to time, any organization has to undergo changes to keep going. When part of an organization does not perform satisfactorily, don't condemn the whole and start to reorganize right away. Instead, try to locate the reasons for the malfunction. Then determine what changes are needed to improve performance. Try to avoid radical reorganization with a sledgehammer so you can avoid the after-effects. Take your scalpel and change only those parts that need to be operated upon. Selective reorganization takes thought and study, but if you make this an on-going evolutionary process, the trauma of an overall reorganization is absent.

If one massive reorganization fails, a manager cannot afford to initiate another immediately. The confidence in her leadership would be shaken even further by creating another period of uncertainty and confusion that a second reorganization would trigger.

The ways to reorganize are many. That's what makes reorganization so risky. You can shift people and responsibilities from box to box on an organization chart in seemingly endless combinations. But such shifting is not a substitute for motivation, leadership, morale, integrity, loyalty, and other qualities that support good staff performance. If only good resulted from reorganization, then box shifting would be an acceptable everyday occurrence. But reorganization affects people deeply. To the affected employee, it's like the events of birth, marriage, and death all rolled into one. So, go easy. You're dealing with people, not boxes. Don't confuse action with progress.

Second in Command

'The measure of man is what he does with power.'
Pittacus

Problem: When Sam became head of his division, he inherited Roger as his deputy chief. Sam had never had a deputy before, so he didn't know exactly how he should use Roger. Sam's uncertainty did not last long, however, because Roger told him exactly how he, Roger, should be used. Roger explained that over the years he had carved out a number of responsibilities for which he was the final division authority. He proposed to continue his role in the same capacity. This way Sam could concentrate on the division's remaining responsibilities. Sam thought this might be all right, but somehow Roger's proposal struck a false note.

Approach: Sam's plight reminds me of an experience I had years ago. I worked for a man who was an engineer by profession. He created a new job in the office that called for a person with a legal background plus managerial experience. He asked me if I would be interested in the job. After I said I would be interested, he told me that he would appoint an engineer to 'share' the job's responsibilities with me and act as my deputy. Although on paper I would be the boss, the deputy would make all the 'technical' decisions and I would make only the legal and administrative decisions.

Without hesitation, I rejected the proposal as unworkable. My common sense told me that only one person can be in charge of an operation. The confusion that results from a bifurcated leadership forms an undesirable operating situation for the staff and for the bifurcated leadership itself. Because my boss urgently needed my abilities in the new position, he did not insist on his plan, but changed his offer to include the condition that an engineer be appointed as my full-time deputy. I had no problem with that proposal. I picked an outstanding engineer whom I really wanted as a deputy, and we worked together amicably and productively without the problem of divided leadership.

Years later, during the 1980 Republican Presidential Nominating Convention in Detroit, the unworkability of 'shared' leadership was driven home to me again. At that convention, former President Gerald Ford surfaced briefly as a possible vice-presidential candidate to run with presidential candidate Ronald Reagan. One of Mr Ford's conditions for acceptance was reported to be that he wished to share certain presidential responsibilities and duties with Mr Reagan in the event they were elected. Mr Reagan quickly rejected this proposal amid an outcry that such an arrangement would weaken and erode the powers of the presidency.

Although organizations are administered in many different ways, the question of who is the final authority in the organization should not be left in doubt. If the overall authority is divided, with a subordinate having decision-making authority not possessed by his boss, a two-headed organization comes into being. Anytime a subordinate has powers not possessed by his boss, the boss is no longer the true boss. 'Who's in charge around here?' becomes a question of reality rather than a joke.

With all the problems that can arise when you appoint a deputy, why have a deputy? That's a question to ask yourself, whether you already have one or are considering the creation of such a position. The value of any position that raises more problems than it solves is questionable, at best. Yet, a good deputy is indispensable.

The ideal deputy serves as a confidant, as a sounding board, as a trouble-shooter, as a special projects person, as a screener, and as an alter ego. He provides leadership continuity and continued stability when the boss is absent. The more he reflects the boss, rather than being different from him, the more predictable is the leadership from the top. If the deputy starts being viewed as one who circumvents the boss and works against him, then the boss – and the organization – are both in trouble. Compatibility of thought and action between a manager and his deputy is critical, and loyalty to each other is their first commandment.

The person who occupies the position of deputy cannot be ambivalent in his loyalty to the boss. A deputy who carps to others about his boss, who second-guesses him, or who sets up his own following is the antithesis of what a good deputy should be. A deputy is invaluable to his boss and the organization, but only if he operates with the highest integrity and support in advancing the goals of his boss. If the deputy cannot, or will not, be supportive of his boss, he should not be in the position of deputy. A deputy's row is tough to hoe, but it can be a very productive one for all if hoed right.

Sick Leave

'Where is everybody?'
Carl Sandburg

Problem: Frank 'just knew' that all of the sick leave taken by his office staff was not legitimate. There were so many instances where an employee looked and acted perfectly healthy one day, reported in sick the next day, and returned to work the following day still looking and acting in good health. Frank believed his staff was taking advantage of him by their excessive sick leave absences, and he didn't like it. It would be calling the employee dishonest, though, to accuse him of faking an illness when he claimed to be sick enough to stay home one day, but not sick enough to go to a doctor.

Approach: Have you ever had Frank's problem? You arrive at the office all set to give dictation to your secretary of some letters that must go out today. But you can't because she doesn't show up. She phoned her best friend in the office a few minutes before you got there to say she wasn't feeling well today. The friend is unable to give you any other details. She does not know how sick your secretary is, what her illness is, or when she plans to return to work.

Sound familiar? This is the usual way that workers notify their office of their absence. You can see why notice is given to a friend. It's easier than talking directly to the boss. Since he usually does not answer the phone himself, it's an uncommon day that the boss gets to talk directly to the 'sick' employee.

Consider the advantages of having the 'sick' employee talk directly to his or her supervisor. The supervisor can ask the general nature of the illness. This helps to determine the length of the absence, so he can plan for possible substitute help. He can ask about pending work that needs reassignment. He can offer whatever help the organization can provide to assist the employee while the illness persists. The main advantage, though, to the organization is to build a sense of accountability into the sick leave process through this form of direct communication.

Think about how you feel on those days when it's tough to get out of bed. If you're not feeling up to par and you have a backlog of sick leave, it's tempting to think of calling your office friend to say you can't make it today. To yourself you think, 'I'll just take it easy and then get around to some of the chores I've been neglecting here at home. So let the office struggle along without me for one day. They'll survive.'

However, if your supervisor required you to call him direct to explain your proposed absence for the day, you'd think twice about staying home. Chances are you would manage to drag yourself into the office rather than fib.

A word of caution about starting the policy of phoning direct to the boss if you or any employee is ill and unable to report for duty unexpectedly. While this policy can be effective in trimming sick leave abuse, it's a difficult one to implement. Unless you persist, it won't work. To chat with an office friend is so much easier than reporting sick to the boss himself, unless one is really sick. Then to report to the boss direct is no problem.

Speaking Up

*'One of the greatest failings of today's executive is
his inability to do what he's supposed to do.'*
                                           Malcolm Kent

Problem: Although Rick encouraged submission of constructive ideas
and suggestions from the employees in his section, he received little
worthwhile feedback from any of them. He did receive occasional
criticism of his management by a few of the staff, but the criticism
failed to be accompanied by suggestions for improvement. It was so
easy to criticize that Rick thought how simple it would be for one of his
employees to get ahead by presenting constructive ideas to better the
section. To better the section was what Rick tried to do all day long.
Why shouldn't the others?

Approach: Rick's employees were no different from employees every-
where. They don't like to rock the boat. They come to work, do their
jobs, and go home. They may or may not like what they are doing, but
they don't want to be too visible to the boss. If they're not sure of
themselves, they feel that establishing their identity with the boss may
expose their weaknesses. If they are sure of themselves, they may not
want to identify their strengths to their boss for fear he might assign
them more work for the same pay.

The lack of employee willingness to take a chance by speaking up to
the boss presents a field day for those who are willing to become visible.
There is little risk in speaking out if an employee has something
worthwhile to say. This goes for managers speaking up to managers
above them as well as for staff employes speaking up to their supervisors. So even though Rick cannot inspire his employees to criticize
constructively, he can understand how frustrated his own boss must be
with the same problem. Rick could turn his thoughts to what he might
suggest to improve the whole department as well as just his own
division.

Speaking up to a boss consists of giving well-considered, constructive opinions on a subject when the timing is right to express such
opinions. To speak up meaningfully requires advance thought on the
subject. Such preparation translates into thinking through what needs
to be brought to the boss's attention for his consideration in making
managerial decisions. It also means viewing the subject from the boss's
vantage point, while projecting pertinent items that you observe from
your own vantage point. It means never attempting to embarrass
the boss or to show him up. This approach makes your comments

constructive as contrasted to the purely negative comments that can be spewed forth effortlessly but which lack the analysis required to suggest improvement. A boss hungers for problem solutions, not criticism without remedies.

Speaking up can be done in person or in writing, depending on the circumstances. I recall speaking up to one of my bosses on the subject of his weekly staff meeting. Frankly, the meetings had become a drag. They were too long, aimless and generally uninspiring. All staff members who attended the meetings had felt this way for some time, but none made their feelings known to the boss. To spare him any possible embarrassment, I decided to write a memorandum to him outlining a suggested format for future staff meetings to replace the wandering 'show and tell' format that dominated the current meetings. I suggested in my memo that the boss consider distributing before each meeting a written agenda showing an estimated time limit for discussion of each item. I suggested that the possible benefits coming from the change would be better use of staff time because of more incisive discussions at the meetings and better followup actions. I closed by saying that he might wish to discuss the staff meeting format with the staff at the next meeting before considering it further. It turned out that the boss welcomed my suggestion because he was no more fond of the existing format than the staff itself.

Once your boss recognizes you offer problem solutions, he will be so receptive to your ideas that he will ask for your suggestions on specific problems. You'll be the type of employee every boss looks for but seldom finds. You will definitely be visible.

The rewards that come when you emerge from the crowd are many. You liberate your mind by sharing it with others. Others will look to you for advice and support. Your boss will know he can depend on you for your straightforwardness, an asset he will treasure. Your real reward will be that of working in an organization with better management, which you helped create.

Speech Making

> *'A speech is a solemn responsibility. The man who makes a bad thirty-minute speech to two hundred people wastes only a half hour of his own time. But he wastes one hundred hours of the audience's time – more than four days – which should be a hanging offence.'*
>
> Jenkin Lloyd Jones

Problem: When he accepted a managerial position, Lonnie knew he would have to present briefings and speeches as chief of his division. Although he did not tell anyone, he felt that this was one of the principal drawbacks to his new job. He feared making a speech – his insides churned up something awful when it was his turn. To avoid his fear, he tried not to think about the speech he was scheduled to give before it was time to deliver it. This method gave him little preparation time for his talk, but it did get the ordeal over more quickly than if he engaged in extensive preparation.

Approach: Since speech making is a part of any manager's job, Lonnie owes it to himself and his job to try to conquer his fear of speaking before a group. A manager's speech making comes in various forms. The morning may find him delivering an informal talk to his staff. The afternoon may find him making a speech to an outside group, or giving a briefing to his boss, or giving a detailed explanation of the functions of his division to another division of the organization. Speech making is more than the formal reading of a prepared text to an audience. That type of speech plays a small role in a manager's life compared with other forms of speech making.

Practically any time you make extended remarks, you make a speech. Even some conversations, particularly those at one-on-one managerial meetings where a problem is discussed between two parties, can fall into the category of speech making.

Speech making offers a platform for managers to get points across that cannot be got across in any other manner. You usually make a speech in one of two possible situations. Either you are invited to make a speech or, as a manager, you invite others to listen to you. This places you in a commanding position. Speech making is done mostly without interruption. This allows the speaker to make his points as tellingly as he is prepared to do. That's the rub. Unless you prepare adequately, you can forfeit the opportunity to make a good presentation. Without preparation, even a speaker well versed in his subject matter can forget major points or wander off course into a sea of verbosity while mentally searching for the points he wishes to make.

What is adequate preparation? First you must know how long your speech is to be and then develop the subject matter to fit that time. You have to know what you want to say and the order in which you want to say it. Even for the simplest speech, some thought and organization are required. For a more complex speech, research may be required as well as subject matter planning and organization. When you think you know what you want to say, write an outline of your speech. This outline may vary in length from a part of a page to several pages, depending on the complexity and length of your speech. But the shorter the outline, the better.

Once you develop your written outline, review it for improvements. Are there additions or deletions you want to make? Does it contain all the points you want to make? Is it free of the extraneous? Will the audience understand it? Is it convincing and persuasive? Does it fit the time requirements? Keep working on the outline until it fulfils your demands of it.

When the outline is finished, close your office door and run through your speech. Deliver it aloud just as though you were speaking before a live audience. Follow your outline. Check your time. Once the dry run is done, revise the speech if needed to meet your criteria. Do at least one additional dry run, preferably more, before you make your actual presentation. This will maximize your familiarity with your outline and will inject a ring of assurance and authority into your speech when you make it. Your audience will know that you take them and your subject seriously.

Following these rules is how I transformed myself from a knee-knocking, stomach-full-of-butterflies speaker into one who came to enjoy, even relish, any form of speech making. I found the way to control the fear factor was never to open my mouth without knowing what I was going to say and why. If you follow these suggestions and still never conquer your fear of public speaking, you'll be in good company. For example, when General Motors Chairman and Chief Executive Officer Thomas A. Murphy retired, he confessed in a *Wall Street Journal* interview that his fear of public speaking was still so great that, in spite of frequent speeches, he bordered on 'becoming physically ill' from pre-speech nervousness.

One final point: slide presentations of statistics during the course of a speech. (My personal preference is for eliminating them completely, but if you are going to use visual aids, do it right.) I have rarely seen a statistical slide add anything to a speech, but I have often seen such slides destroy the effectiveness of an otherwise good speech. Besides the seemingly inevitable problems with faulty projectors, poor lighting, crowded charts, and unreadable slides, bare statistics slides usually are boring. If statistics are pertinent don't be so lazy as to expect your audience to understand them without help. Make all visuals clear, crisp, and readable. Do everything possible to be sure that lighting will be sufficient and that all equipment will be in good working order. Don't simply use the statistics as a visual crutch. Refer to the slides and work the statistics into your talk by interpreting them for your audience. Make the statistical information come alive with meaning so that they will add to your talk, not detract from it.

Staff Activity Reports

'And in today already walks tomorrow.'
Samuel Taylor Coleridge

Problem: In her new job as section manager, Anna became frustrated with her inability to keep track of the progress of significant activities within her section. Most of the important activities were completed actions by the time they reached her. She believed that some of the activities should not have been pursued at all, while others should have been developed more thoroughly. But entering into a perpetual second-guessing game would not solve anything. She decided that she would be unable to influence the direction of her section's activities until she had a system that kept her on top of the initiation and the progress of the more important work efforts of her section.

Approach: Keeping abreast of progress towards objectives in the organization is not an option for a manager. It is a must. Some managers do this by relying on informal oral staff reports; others lean towards written reports or formal briefings. Most rely on a combination of these communication techniques.

A manager's ability to sort out the significant from the superfluous is fundamental to the productive use of her time. Knowing what is significant helps a manager to spot trends in productivity so that she can emphasize development of a good trend and re-direct a poor one.

One device to keep track of trends – and to know about those parts of the organization doing significant things and those parts doing not so significant things – is to require each supervisor who reports to you to submit an activity report each week. The report sums up important events of the past week and projects important actions coming up in the week ahead. Insist on no more than a few items and limit each item to a short paragraph. Otherwise, the length of the report will prevent you from reading it quickly. If nothing significant occurred and no important projects are anticipated for the reporting period for any unit, a negative report should be submitted.

After I launched such a system of reporting in my office, it quickly became part of the routine. When my secretary received the items from the staff, she consolidated them and placed the report on my desk by eleven o'clock every Friday, without fail, whether or not I was in the office that day. Rarely would the consolidated report exceed one typewritten page.

I found out that, before I requested these weekly reports, the managers of units under me did not always know the status of work in their units. When I instigated my weekly status report, the unit managers had to ask for similar reports from their workers so that they could comply with my request. At first glance, this may seem to be just one more series of reports – an increase in paperwork, when everyone knows there's too much already. But these status reports proved a boon to me and to the managers under me because the reports helped us to monitor the progress of the work of the division.

This type of report almost provides a manager with a weekly snapshot of her staff and its work. It shows what is considered important and by whom. It was a report that I could read in its entirety in a few minutes. It inspired me to follow up on some points and to do some long-range planning on others, as well as some redirection where required. It presented me with a capsule analysis of the organization's week-to-week work through the eyes of my highest supervisors. It made my staff think about the progress of their units before preparing their reports. If a supervisor failed to submit reports of significant items for any length of time, it gave both him and me a communication on the management of that particular unit. In effect, the reports drew a profile of the organization's work progress.

I find that the problem with most reports is finding time to read and grasp the amount of detail included and then, if required, to try to do something about the activity, unless, as so many reports indicate, further action is preempted because the course of action is 'locked in'. A brief weekly report of past and projected actions avoids these problems.

To demonstrate how such a report can benefit you, here's a sample of the types of items that might be submitted by one of your units:

PROJECTED ACTION
Bill Larson and Helen Marks plan to meet again next Thursday with Acme representatives to determine what can be done to get the contract with them back on schedule. If the meeting is unproductive, an immediate decision will have to be made on whether to place a hold on the company's pending request for payment.

PAST ACTION
John Hanrahan's Denver recruiting trip exceeded expectations. Three hiring commitments were made. More commitments could have been made if more positions were available for filling.

You can see the possibilities for potential action by you in this example. In announcing your desire for such a report, be certain to cite your own examples of the type of items you will expect to receive each week. As examples, consider using recent past and projected actions that you wish you'd known about sooner so that you might have had at least the opportunity to provide some influence on the final outcome.

Standup Meetings

'Some people feel with their heads and think with their hearts.'
G. C. Lichtenberg

Problem: Every so often some event occurred in Charley's division that made him feel exuberant. While this feeling still possessed him, he'd mention the good news to whoever happened to be near him at the time and then he'd go back to work. Occasionally it occurred to him that he'd like to share the joy of the event with his entire staff, but that was impossible because of the difficulty of obtaining a meeting room on short notice and getting everyone together at one time.

Approach: A manager's sharing of happy news immediately with his staff can add an unusual manager-staff dimension to an organization. That's when a standup meeting is in order, and that's what Charley can do to overcome the meeting barriers that he's constructed in his mind.

A standup meeting is what its name implies. It is a meeting, an impromptu one, where everyone remains standing, including the boss. A standup meeting works well when there's good news to report. Serious topics, lectures, or announcing policy changes are not meant for a standup meeting.

A standup meeting might be triggered when you receive news that one of your employees has been selected for an important award. Other standup meeting possibilities could be for news of a big promotion, a unique staff accomplishment, or to squelch a troublesome rumour. Associating a standup meeting with 'good' things sets a mood of gaiety and conjecture before the subject is announced. It's like your own little festival. It also is one of the few times that the entire staff – typists, secretaries, file clerks, supervisors, and professionals – will rub shoulders for a common meeting. This makes the meeting special in itself.

A typical standup meeting can take place within a matter of minutes from conception to finish. When you get some really good news that spurs you on to hold such a meeting, have your secretary notify the staff that you are going to have such a meeting and ask them to congregate outside your office in fifteen minutes. Keep the subject a surprise. Those who can break away from what they are doing will be there. Those who cannot will understand that their presence is not mandatory. One of the good features of a standup meeting is that you don't wait until everyone can attend. By then the glow may be off. So, do it when the subject is hot and the spirit is right. It's spontaneous and from the heart. Momentarily, the organization is welded together a little more closely.

Staying Accessible

'Never less alone than when alone.'
Samuel Rogers

Problem: Before Robert became a supervisor, he was able to work a project through to completion. There were interruptions, but the interruptions hadn't dominated his day as they had since he had become manager. He decided that the only way he could be sure of any time to himself was to block out a part of the day when no interruptions would be allowed. Each morning he closed his door until noon with instructions that he was not to be disturbed for any reason except, of course, a call from either his boss or his wife. Before long, he had few interruptions, morning or afternoon. Hardly anyone consulted him with any regularity.

Approach: If you find yourself empathizing with Robert – that is, if you want an abundance of quietude – then, for you, being a manager can be difficult. Solitude, time to think, and peace and quiet are all required to be a good manager, but in a manager's job they come in small doses.

Unless a manager remains accessible to his staff, to outside callers, to his boss, and to the assorted interrupters seeking his attention during a normal day, he'll soon find that his presence or absence is not very relevant.

If you adopt a closed-door policy, designate only certain hours when you can be interrupted or seen, require an appointment for every staff discussion, routinely refer most telephone calls and outside visitors to someone else, the word will spread that you don't want to be bothered by much of anything. In no time at all, your part of the organization will be run by others. The overall management of your office will develop a helter-skelter pattern as you insulate yourself from the goings-on of the very organization you're supposed to be directing. You'll get free time, but you won't be managing. To manage, you have to involve yourself. Otherwise, you lose touch with and control of your organization.

Accessibility fosters understanding. Understanding fosters better management, because to make decisions and give direction, a manager has to know what's going on. Inaccessibility leads to a cloistered existence. That may be fine in a monastery, but in an office it's a disaster. Remember, accessibility doesn't mean that a manager drops whatever he is doing for every interruption. Accessibility, like all managerial functions, involves a decision-making process. Let people know that you are accessible. Then it's up to you to evaluate each request for your time.

126

Be alert for signs of how others view your accessibility. You may regard yourself as an accessible manager, but those wanting to talk with you or correspond with you may not agree. If you're consistently hard to reach by phone, if you don't return your calls promptly or, worse yet, fail to return some calls at all, you're sending a message that you don't want to get involved. Ultimately, those persons who get that message may decide that they can find their answers elsewhere. Similarly, you will alienate those persons to whom you do not respond when they write to you or ask to meet with you. The same negative picture of you can be projected without your cognizance by an over-protective secretary. Her interceptions of requests for your time may be well-meaning, but they can cut you off from important contacts. Double-check your own accessibility practices and those of persons close to you in your office, and if you find you are plagued by any or all of these shields to your accessibility, start your reentry process by taking the steps needed to remove or lower the shields.

Training

'Sixty years ago I knew everything; now I know nothing; education is a progressive discovery of our own ignorance.'

Will Durant

Problem: Jane had been trying for years to better herself by enrolling in management training courses offered by her employer. She was not a manager herself, but she believed that such courses would help her overcome limitations in her background so she would qualify to fill a managerial vacancy. The training courses helped little because, although no boss had ever been truthful with her when she was turned down for managerial jobs, Jane's personal deficiencies caused her applications to be turned down for managerial positions. When Mark became Jane's new boss, Jane asked him to send her to yet another training course. She said that if he refused, he would be holding her back from pursuing her management career goals.

Approach: As a new manager, Mark has to face up to one more problem he did not have while he was in the ranks. That is, how much benefit is derived from employee training courses? Such evaluation is an elusive managerial problem. In some organizations, there is so much training available, so many persons pushing courses, and so many pressures to give employees training that it is hard for a manager to translate the value received from training into specific job requirements.

You have to be especially nimble-footed to side-step the trap of giving your employees training just for the sake of saying that they have had training. This is a pitfall in those organizations that employ staff training officers. A training officer's job is to ensure that employees attend training courses. He is not concerned with problems in your office caused by the absence of the employee who is attending a course. You can't quibble with the training officer about his attitude, but you still have the problem of your boss demanding more production while one or more of your workers is off on a couple of weeks training.

To both control and encourage needed staff training, a manager should periodically survey the training needs of his staff. First have your supervisors meet individually with their staffs to assess the training needs and desires of each employee for a period of a year. Such a sit-down session provides an opportunity for a supervisor and an employee to discuss and tailor a training needs package that looks to the employee's immediate needs and to his career objectives. This procedure helps to curb the 'training for training's sake' attitude that training officers promote to fulfil their quotas. After the inventory of training needs is complete, work with the training officer to obtain the courses necessary to fill the needs if such courses are not already available.

It's wise to require that each training course be evaluated by those in attendance and that those evaluations be made available to you. Review of these opinions will allow you to adjust or redirect training for your employees. The best-sounding course in the world may turn out to be less than worthwhile and you ought to know about its shortcomings. If you have a problem getting the results of an evaluation from the training officer (and you may if adverse comments were made by the students), design a course evaluation sheet yourself. Ask each of your employees to return the completed sheet to you through his supervisor after completion of the course.

If your survey of training needs doesn't turn up a request for a personal development course, such as 'Getting Along with People', or 'Getting to Know Yourself', request such a course. These courses concentrate on individual personal and interpersonal development as opposed to the technicalities of, say, automatic data processing. Enrol yourself, along with others on your staff. In a good course, you'll benefit by the things you learn about yourself and about the people who work with you. During the course you'll find yourself viewed by some of your employees in an entirely different light – that of a human being with the same needs and wants as those of your staff members.

Turf Battles

'It is a curious fact that of all the illusions that beset mankind none is quite so curious as that tendency to suppose that we are mentally and morally superior to those who differ from us in opinion.'

Elbert Hubbard

Problem: Joan couldn't believe what was happening to her. Worse yet, she didn't know what to do about it, and even if she did, she wasn't sure she had the stomach for fighting for her 'rights'. Since becoming division chief she thought that she had established a close working relationship with her fellow division chiefs. They had seemed very understanding and helpful to her as she tried to gain managerial experience. Now this. When she arrived at work this morning, she found a note from her boss asking for comments on a proposal from another division chief requesting that a major part of the work of Joan's division be transferred to his division. The reasons for the transfer sounded logical and compelling in light of the production problems she was having with this part of her division. She felt very much on the defensive against such an experienced division chief.

Approach: Joan is in for an even greater emotional shock in this, her first managerial 'turf battle'. To explain the depth of emotions evoked by a turf battle to a person who has never engaged in one takes some doing. A turf battle is a fight over who should have jurisdiction over a certain responsibility. Both participants want the authority. Organizations always have responsibilities that could be located logically in any one of several divisions. The decision as to which department was given the jurisdiction originally was probably made arbitrarily by the boss at the time. Since there is as much 'logic' for the disputed responsibility to be in one division as the other, its final resting place may depend on which manager musters the most arguments in the loudest voice.

You don't have to be a manager to be involved in a turf battle, of course, but the stakes are higher when you are because more than your own personal interest is affected by the outcome. If you lose, a part of your organization may be wiped out and an important responsibility transferred to someone else. If you win, you may end up merely even or you may wind up with more responsibility than you had before the battle began.

Assuming you are not the initiator, a typical turf battle for you starts when one of your peers decides that something you are responsible for ought to be the responsibility of his organization. In his first skirmish on the proposed takeover of your turf, you should expect little or no warning. If he's a veteran turf battler, he won't warn you in the slightest. Naturally, he'll expect to catch you flatfooted. Turf battles are a nasty business.

Although your natural instincts of the jungle will come to your aid, there are some basic rules to be followed if you are challenged and expect to hold your own. These are:

1. Commit yourself firmly to your position to keep your ground.
2. Tell your opponent of your commitment and otherwise work to convince him that you are a 'match' for him in this battle. Don't negotiate with him.
3. Cry 'foul' loudly to your boss and express your commitment to him.
4. Convince everyone else of your commitment – you're in the battle to stay.
5. Go all out to win. Marshal all logical arguments for retaining the responsibility, including those connected with the high cost of moving it. (Bosses are always sensitive to 'cost' arguments.)
6. Initiate your own turf battle with your opponent if the battle seems to be going in his favour. Demand jurisdiction over at least one of his responsibilities. Marshal equally logical arguments for such a transfer as you did for keeping the responsibility that he's trying to take away from you.

Having logic on your side is helpful, but logic is only part of the story. Your determination not to be defeated by below-the-belt tactics of a peer is of great importance. In that sense, it's an alley fight. If you are scuttled by a peer, you'll find that for the moment you're no longer a peer. Vigorous resistance of the takeover, therefore, even if you do lose, is essential to prevent further takeover battles.

Unfortunately, turf battles, as disconcerting and acrimonious as they may seem, have to be faced if you are going to run an organization. If you get a reputation for turning the other cheek, you'll invite more forays into your territory. If you lose a few of these battles, you won't be much of a manager because you won't have much left to manage. If you can earn a reputation for being someone who shouldn't be tangled with, you'll minimize the number of turf battles you're subjected to. And then you can devote your time trying to run a better organization, free from the hard feelings generated by turf battles.

Visibility

Problem: When Carolyn was promoted out of the ranks to become division chief a year ago, she knew everyone in the division. In addition to knowing what tasks they performed, she knew about the major happenings in their personal lives. They, too, knew as much about her. But that changed after her promotion. With new responsibilities, she became tied to her desk, and the occasions for talking personally to more than a handful of her staff were few. As old employees left and new ones were hired, her personal associations with the staff became even more remote. She missed the old closeness but did not know how to reestablish it.

Approach: Any new boss, like Carolyn, has new problems to face, but how to project one's own personality may be one of the most challenging. A boss can, if she likes, make a career of being largely invisible to her working staff. Physically invisible, that is. She may be highly visible through written directives and memos, but not through her physical presence. Invisibility occurs when a manager deals with the bulk of her employees mainly through their supervisors, who report to her. From a time and effectiveness standpoint, it's not possible for a manager to directly supervise more than a handful of employees. That's why a supervisory structure exists. It's a way of getting the job done. It's also a way of making yourself invisible to much of your staff.

In this age of real and imagined impersonalness, the boss who refuses to shroud herself in a veil of physical invisibility can create awareness of herself that's beneficial to both herself and her staff. The easiest way to mix with the staff is to take time to walk through the office at least once each day. Vary the time of day that you tour so that you can catch the different moods of the office.

Several benefits result from this managerial visibility. The staff gets familiar with your presence. This helps to lessen the tension at other times whenever a staff member has to meet with you personally. The rank-and-file staff knows you exist and are not a figurehead grinding out written directives for them to implement. You become an individual, not just a name on a memo. You can exchange greetings with them, and they can tell you things you might otherwise not learn.

Intangible benefits are added to your managerial strength. You see your staff under actual working conditions. You pick up the 'feel' of various parts of the office. If people in one part of the office are usually

133

chatting and those in another part are usually engrossed in their work, you can question why there is a difference. Don't jump to the conclusion beforehand that the chatters do not accomplish as much as the others. But if you do walk around each day and observe, you see an office profile that you would not see otherwise. Because better working conditions and office space are always high on the 'wish' list, you get a close view of these conditions. During your tours, you can extend a compliment, note a new hair style, learn of a wedding, birth, holiday, and the other events that comprise the personal lives of your staff.

Your walk-throughs help to open up the office from the top. They add something personal to the routine of the day for both you and your staff, but mostly you express your awareness of the office and your accessibility to the staff instead of fostering that austere managerial attitude that promotes hostility.

Watching Your Words

*'Man does not live by words alone, despite the fact
that sometimes he has to eat them.'*
                                        Adlai Stevenson

Problem: Jerry fumed as he finished the report prepared for him by
Leslie. As division head, Jerry saw Leslie very little since she was fairly
well down the line. Still, this was the second recent piece of work she
had done unsatisfactorily. As he put the report aside, he noticed Leslie's
supervisor nearby and shouted to him, 'What's the matter with Leslie?
Can't she do anything right?' He made these remarks half in anger and
half in hope that Leslie's boss would take heed and admonish Leslie. He
didn't realize that several of Leslie's co-workers were also within
earshot.

Approach: Jerry forgot that practically everything a boss says is passed
on to the staff. And that's what you should remember whenever you
say anything in connection with your job as manager. Assume that
whatever you say will be passed on and possibly, nay probably, altered
in the process. The staff is always looking for tidbits of information and
gossip through which to shape and re-shape their reactions to management, which is personified by you, the boss, in the front office. Your
attitude affects the attitude of the whole office, so be careful what you
say and where you say it.
   If a boss criticizes one member of his staff to another, consider it, ipso
facto, that the criticism will be communicated to the person being
criticized. If that is the boss's aim, that's one thing. No matter, the
effect of the boss's words will come back to him in one form or another.
The subject of the criticism may confront you and demand an explanation, or he may intentionally bog down his work and thus affect the
production of the entire office. The office will take sides, and many
members of the staff will be with the employee and against you if only
because of the human tendency to root for the underdog.
   So, as inviting as it may seem at the time, engaging in this type of
personal criticism constitutes a destructive managerial method. First
of all, it's unfair for a boss, with all of his power, to ever 'pick on' an
employee, but to do so by an indirect means is a gross misuse of power.
Furthermore, even if criticism is warranted, it will be garbled by the
time it reaches the employee and your message will not be communicated properly. This, on top of the humiliation the employee will
suffer, negates any possible improvement you may have hoped to
engender.

If an employee needs to be reprimanded or criticized in your estimation, then bring the matter to the employee's attention in an unemotional manner. If the employee is not under your direct supervision, attack the problem through the chain of command to determine how the employee's work can be improved. Get the chain hopping on what went wrong and how it can be prevented from happening again. Perhaps the employee never got the project instructions you delineated. If not, why not? Can the project be salvaged?

While a boss must, in fairness, harness his inclination to criticize his employees, this does not imply that he must completely suppress his emotions. But, like all things, the excesses must be guarded against. Otherwise 'How do I get out of this place?' may become the office theme song instead of 'I enjoy working here.'

Working While Commuting

'Do what you can, with what you have, where you are.'
Theodore Roosevelt

Problem: During his forty-minute bus ride back and forth from the office each day, Wes acted like most other passengers. He disconnected his brain and waited for the ride to end. A few people read newspapers, but most stared ahead blankly for the entire trip. Since Wes had been promoted to section chief, he considered the bus ride a bigger waste of time than ever. In the morning he was anxious for the trip to end so he could begin work. On the trip home at night, he was equally anxious for the trip to end so he could eat dinner and start on the backlog of work he brought with him from the office.

Approach: If you're lucky enough to ride on good public transport and to be able to get a seat for the whole trip back and forth each day, you can chip away at some of your office work without lengthening your work day. If Wes thought about it, he would see that using his riding time is as good as finding an extra hour or so a day to keep up with his job's demands.

Trains, buses, and planes are great places to catch up on the reading matter that has piled up in the office. There are no telephone calls or other office-type interruptions. Moreover, the fact that you know the trip takes a fixed amount of time makes you concentrate harder. If you plough through accumulated reading matter on public transport, you make efficient use of your travelling time.

Because of the jerky motions of trains and buses, they are difficult places to do legible writing. However, planes and airport terminals are excellent places to do office-related writing as well as reading. Make it a habit to carry more than enough writing and reading material so that you can take advantage of delays encountered in air travel. Plane terminals also offer fairly private phone cubby holes so you can catch up on calls.

During daylight hours you can even insulate yourself from watching the dramatics involved in wild cab rides to and from airports to concentrate on your reading. In addition to getting the work done, you'll give your blood pressure a lift by ignoring all the traffic accidents your cab almost has.

You'll have to train yourself to become adept at reading or studying on public transport. But if you don't succeed at first, don't give up. Such vehicles are noisy from engine and people sounds, are not well lighted, and have that constant jerky motion. Once you overcome the hurdle of these disturbances, you have access to a slice of time that you come to depend on. In what otherwise might be a monotonous, nonproductive ride, you'll discover yourself looking forward to the ride so you can use your bonus time.

Years ago, when I began taking rather frequent early morning business flights, I developed a study habit that still persists. I discovered that by arriving at the airline terminal an hour or an hour and a half before flight time, I could settle down to an intensive review of the subject that was the purpose of my trip. Then, after breakfasting during the flight, I could go over my material one more time. This ritual of eleventh-hour study so polishes my knowledge of the subject and bolsters my self-confidence for the conference ahead that these pre-dawn risings are bearable.

Your Personal Career Management

*'I am a great believer in luck, and I find the harder
I work the more I have of it.'*

Thomas Jefferson

Problem: Kim dedicated herself to her work and always did her best,
whatever the assignment. Not the most outstanding employee on the
staff, she was, however, a dependable, solid worker. She received
several promotions during the five years she had been with the organization, even though she had not sought them. Her bosses had recognized that she assumed additional job responsibilities and rewarded her
efforts accordingly. She prided herself on the fact that she had never
asked for a promotion and that she hadn't job hopped as some of her
associates had. She had no idea of where she wanted to be on the job
ladder in the next five years, but she was confident that she would
progress as well as she had in the past.

Approach: Doing the best job you can has rewards as Kim experienced.
But sometimes, like virtue, the accomplishment itself may be the only
reward. Following the suggestions in this book can help you be a better
manager, but you could be the best manager this world has ever seen
and still go nowhere. There are bosses who do not bestow promotions,
however much warranted. Bosses, such as Kim's, who do promote
deserving employees, are not just being altruistic. Each one is acting
first for his own benefit. He *needs* the ability of the good employee in a
higher position. But waiting for the boss to recognize that he needs to
promote you, if only to help himself, makes your career progress
unnecessarily haphazard.

The key to a successful career for yourself is taking charge of that
career. You can't leave this to others. Just working hard and leaving
your advancement to others, as Kim does, is a career plan of sorts, you
might say. But can you be sure that others can plan your career better
than you? In some instances, of course, you can ride the coattails of a
boss on his way up and conceivably end up with an impressive career.
But that is leaving much to chance. There is a better way.

First, analyse your present job. Are you in a dead-end position? Are
you in a job where you cannot utilize all your skills and talents? Is your
job a bore? Is your firm retrenching or, worse yet, on the verge of
bankruptcy? While you can't control these negative circumstances,
you can still exert control over your career.

After you analyse your present job, evaluate how much you like it
and where it can lead. Is this where you want to go? If not, where do you

want to be in a year, two years, five years, ten years, and at the end of your working career? What do you want to do with your life? What are your interests? What motivates you? What are your skills? What job or career embodies most of the things you enjoy?

Once you can visualize your career goal, the next step is to analyse what you need to do to achieve that goal. Do you need additional training or formal schooling to get where you want to be? Can you get this schooling in your home town or by correspondence? If not, how far do you have to travel to secure it? How much are you willing to sacrifice to get where you want to go? Is your goal realistic?

From the answers you give yourself, formulate a career plan. Of course, there are uncertainties, but you can anticipate the basic variables of the future and think of alternate routes as you plan. Formulation of your career plan may well be the hardest task you ever face. But if you don't take the time to plan, your career will be one that develops by default.

No matter where you now are in your life, design a roadmap setting forth where you want to go and list what it takes to get there. Be specific. Set deadlines for completion of the steps. Put your plan into effect and monitor your progress as you go along. If the deadlines you set are not met, determine why. Modify your plan as circumstances and your objectives change. Some objectives at age twenty-one may have evaporated by the time you reach a more mature age, but this is no cause for alarm. Such a change may only mark your growth as a person, so alter your plan to fit that growth. Career charting for a lifetime demands a flexible plan.

Remember that your plan has to be more than a vague hope of 'being successful'. After you have carefully mapped out your plan, you have to implement it each working day. If you continue to work in a field you don't like, or for a boss who does not appreciate you, or in a job that does not use your skills, no fairy godmother will swoop down to lift you out of your morass. Only you can do that. Knowing where you want to go and how you are going to get there through your career plan will help you get back on track when necessary. If you have to job-hop or ask your boss for a rise to stay on your career path, do it. To manage your career successfuly constitutes the ultimate in solving a management problem.

And in Conclusion . . .

'Few people think more than two or three times a year. I have made an international reputation for myself by thinking once or twice a week.'

George Bernard Shaw

The problems I have discussed in this book are only some of those a manager may expect to encounter during his career. Of course, not all possible problems have been covered since that would be impossible for any book. Nevertheless, a pattern emerges from the illustrations that should become ingrained in a manager's thought processes so that he follows that pattern whenever he is faced with a management problem, whether discussed in this book or not. Following that pattern becomes almost a knee-jerk reaction.

Analyse the problem: When a problem arises or, better yet, when you sense that it may develop, analyse what the problem is all about. How does the troublesome area differ from the ideal? What is happening that should not be happening and what is not happening that should be? What caused the problem? Who is responsible for letting it become a problem? Can it be prevented? Is it serious enough to worry about? What will happen if no change is made?

Consider solutions to the problem: After you know the origin of, and the reasons for, the problem, analyse possible solutions. Assess the pros and cons of all these possibilities. Which promises the greatest gain and incurs the smallest loss? Which proposed solution shows the most consideration for the feelings of the persons primarily affected? Which solution appears to be the one that will endure the longest – that is, which appears to be the best in the long run? Which one do you feel the most comfortable with?

Decide on a solution and implement it: Discuss the choices with the staff members who are affected and decide on a solution and implement it. Try to evoke staff support, but don't be discouraged if the solution you select is not popular, so long as you're convinced that it is the right one. Remember that it can get mighty lonely at the top at times, and this can be one of those times.

Control progress of the solution after implementation: Once the solution has been implemented, monitor the direction the change in procedure takes so you can be sure that it goes the way you want it to go. If there's a hitch, redirect the procedure towards the goal you have set. If a fair trial shows that the solution you picked is not working, don't be bull-headed. Return to the drawing board for a new plan. In the management field, hardly anything turns out to be perfect. It's just that some things work better than others. Keep striving for the solution that works the best.

Finally, be fair, be courteous, be sincere, be courageous. Maintain your balance and common sense, and you'll help others maintain theirs. Don't be afraid to be the boss. Enjoy it. Your attitude will show and be appreciated by those under you and those over you in the organization.

About the Author

James O. McDonald completed the writing of this book in San Diego, California, where he now lives. He was born in Schenectady, New York, and has lived and worked in many places throughout the United States. He received a Bachelor of Arts degree from Syracuse University, a Juris Doctor degree from DePaul University College of Law, and a Certificate from the Environmental Management Institute of the University of Southern California. He has been a sports-writer, a soldier, a governmental administrator, and an attorney included in *Who's Who in American Law*. No matter what his occupation at the time, he always considers himself a manager, a person who likes to get things done. While serving as an enforcement administrator with the US Environmental Protection Agency, he was the first person in the history of the Agency to win its two top honour awards, the Gold Medal for Exceptional Service and the Gold Medal for Distinguished Service. John Quarles, in his book, *Cleaning up America*, credited McDonald with providing 'the leadership to build a nationwide EPA enforcement effort'. In 1980, the Lake Michigan Federation presented him with the Rachel Carson Great Lakes Award for his significant contribution to the preservation of the Lakes. During the course of his career, his accomplishments have been reported on network television news programmes and in major newspapers.